Parenting & Partnering
with Purpose

Parenting & Partnering *with* Purpose

Linking Homes, Schools and Churches
to Educate Our Children

NATALIE A. FRANCISCO, ED. D.

PARENTING AND PARTNERING WITH PURPOSE: Linking Homes, Schools and Churches to Educate Our Children

Cover Design by Atinad Designs

© Copyright 2010

SAINT PAUL PRESS, DALLAS, TEXAS

First Printing, 2010

All rights reserved. No part of this publication may be reproduced, stored in a retrieval system, or transmitted in any form or by any means, electronic, mechanical, photocopying, recording, or otherwise, without the prior permission of the copyright owner, except for brief quotations included in a review of the book.

The name SAINT PAUL PRESS and its logo are registered as a trademark in the U.S. patent office.

ISBN-13: 978-0-9826196-3-6

Printed in the U.S.A.

Dedication

TO MY DAUGHTERS: Nicole, Lesley and Lauren, without whom my life would have been absent of inexpressible joy and incomprehensible juxtapositions because you are the marvelous meshing together of your father and me. You are true gifts from God and our reward.

To my mother, the late Mildred S. Gatling—the consummate teacher and nurturer to my siblings and me. I remember and learn from you even still, although I miss you more than my mind can fathom and my heart can endure.

To the administration, faculty, staff, student body and parents of Calvary Christian Academy for conducting the research and putting forth the effort via administration, teaching, training and a myriad of things too numerous to name. It has been worth the journey because of the quality of staff, students and programs CCA has offered since 1991.

And finally, to my husband and Pastor, Bishop L. W. Francisco III: thank you for entrusting me with the charge to serve as co-founder of CCA. I would have never launched out on my own to take on this challenge of what would become such a magnificent blessing. Only God and you together could accomplish such a feat!

Endorsements

It is an honor and a privilege to present this scholarly and principle-packed work of literature and study. Whether you are a pastor, an educator, administrator, or a parent, you will find this book to be masterfully written to speak to areas of concern or questions you may have regarding parenting and education. My wife has taken her 25 years of parenting and educational experience to present to you a well crafted manual for life and legacy. I know you will be blessed beyond your expectations as you use this valuable resource to perfect your parenting and educational endeavors. This is an absolute must read for everyone concerned about the future of our children."

—Bishop L. W. Francisco III, Senior Pastor
Calvary Community Church, Hampton, VA
Founder, Calvary Christian Academy
& Calvary Covenant Ministries, Inc.
Author, *The 21st Century Man* (St. Paul Press)

Let the Old School principal of the "Three R's" meet the New School Superintendent of the "Three P's!" Dr. Natalie Francisco in her recent literary work, *Parenting and Partnering with Purpose*, takes to task the public, the parish, and the parent for the role each has played in hastening the demise of quality education in our country. Dr. Francisco is well qualified to offer this well documented critique since she is no novice to initiating cutting edge, Christocentric methodology in the classroom.

However, this book is more than a critique of an age-old problem; Dr. Natalie offers tried and true solutions. This book is a must-read for any pastor, parent, educator, or school administrator who is serious about preparing our children to have dominion over an increasingly hostile and agnostic world.

—Rev. Connie J. Jackson
CEO, J. Trinity Communications, Inc.

Dr. Natalie Francisco has done it again! This book is a must read for anyone who is serious and sincere regarding the education of our children. Francisco offers an awesome educational paradigm that blends church, home, school and community together for the synergistic effort of helping children gain a quality education. With the problems that perpetually plague public education systems such as secular humanism and The No Child Left Behind Act which has proven time and again to be insufficient, the information shared within this book is life changing. Thank you, Dr. Francisco, for being a catalyst and conduit of blessing for the nation!

—Dr. John Adolph, author and senior pastor of
Antioch Missionary Baptist Church,
Beaumont, TX

Working under the premise, "It takes a whole village to raise a child," Dr. Natalie A. Francisco writes a book that challenges parents, educators and the Church to step up our game as it relates to the development of our children. This simple and yet profound book is based on the mandate of the Master to "go into all the world and make disciples." Dr. Francisco helps us see that the place to begin is in the inner-city, among the least of these, the hurting masses. Making disciples means meeting people at the point of their need. One does not have to figure out how to do this, because the author has given us a detailed plan and instructions. If we just read, study and practice the principles shared in *Parenting and Partnering with Purpose*, we truly will be the parents, educators and Church that God intends for us to be. And, the lives of people will be transformed.

—Rev. Dr. Cynthia L. Hale, Senior Pastor
Ray of Hope Christian Church
Decatur, GA

Natalie Francisco does a remarkable job of highlighting the proverbial saying, "It Takes a Village to Raise a Child." She clearly conveys the relevance of connecting three vital sectors of society to create an effective and holistic approach to education. This book is a must read for all parents, educators and church leaders.

—Wanda Bolton-Davis, LMSW, M.Div., Author, Speaker
Executive Director of Victorious Disciples Ministries, Inc.
Pastor of Discipleship of St. John Baptist Church,
Grand Prairie and Southlake, TX

Contents

Introduction..15

CHAPTER 1 The Philosophy of Education:
           Two Differing Views..........................19

CHAPTER 2 Demographic Trends and Urban,
           African-American Dilemmas................29

CHAPTER 3 A Parent's Mentoring Mandate....................39

CHAPTER 4 More Parent-Child Strategies....................47

CHAPTER 5 Partnering with Public and Private
           School Educators..............................55

CHAPTER 6 The Responsibility of the Church................63

CHAPTER 7 Establishing a Christian Day Care Center
           and School....................................81

        Counting the Cost..................................83

        Information for Religiously Exempt
        Centers..87

        Choosing a Curriculum..............................89

Setting Policies and Procedures..................91

Evaluating Faculty..95

Administration and Management............100

Summary..111

Bibliography..119

Acknowledgements

IT IS MY belief that all knowledge, wisdom, and understanding come from God, and certainly the ability to apply all three in the rearing of children is most effective when we consult the blueprint of the Holy Bible for handling all of life's issues. As a wife, mother, educator, ordained minister, author, and business woman, I would be remiss to think that who I am and what I have accomplished thus far would have been possible without relying relentlessly on God and the power of His Spirit at work within, for guidance coupled with much faith. I depend upon Him for my spiritual and physical sustenance, and learned to do so because my life's work began at such a young age.

Can you imagine being married at age eighteen and having three children by the age of twenty-six? Along with that, I assumed the roles of volunteering at my daughter's school, working in full-time ministry (without full-time compensation at the time) and pursuing my education through the doctoral level. Yet, in the midst of what seemed like mayhem at times, I am most thankful for the years of love, learning and laughter that came from our household as my husband and I directed and disciplined our three daughters. Because of God's grace and the foundational principles upon which we based our lives, we have reared three well-rounded, intelligent young ladies to our utter delight—and they all love God and are striving to honor Him and serve others with their gifts and talents. What parent could ask for more?

Some would say that the eldest child has the most pressure placed upon him or her because of being the first: the first to be born, the first to learn the ways and wonders of being an only child (for a time), the first to receive discipline, the first to date, and so on. Nicole, our eldest, rose to the challenge of not only being the first in receiving our lessons of life, but she also stepped up to the plate to be a wonderful example to her sisters, and they are still willingly following her today, while embracing their own uniqueness and individuality. Nicole was also the first to say, "Mom, I am not getting married or having any children until you write a book that tells everything you instilled in us." Although I cannot share an exhaustive volume of everything that I've said and done in partnership with my husband, I can give a general overview of the foundational principles and values by which we reared our children and established Calvary Christian Academy, the first African-American owned and operated private Christian school located on the peninsula of the Hampton Roads, Virginia area. To God is the glory for the ability to write and publish this second book!

To that end, I extend my sincere appreciation to St. Paul Press Publishers and every online and brick-and-mortar retail store that carry this book so that parents and educators in both the public and private sector can partner together with the purpose of producing excellent students with the moral conscience and character to leave an indelible mark upon their generation that will not be erased.

Introduction

GOD HAS A perfect plan for the family according to His Word. Husbands and wives are called to operate not independently, but interdependently as the two become "one flesh" in the holy institution of marriage (Matthew 19:5-6). Mothers and fathers are instructed to train up their children in the way they should go (Proverbs 22:6), and children are admonished to honor their parents (Deuteronomy 5:16). Those who are single and widowed are also included in God's plan so that absolutely no one is left out (Psalm 68:6 & 1 Timothy 5:4).

I believe that God desires for us to experience an abundant quality of life as translated by the Greek word **perissos** in John 10:10, which means: *superabundant in quantity or superior in quality; exceeding abundantly above, more abundantly, very highly, beyond measure, more, superfluous.* This kind of life is to be experienced in all of our relationships with God and others. This book will focus on experiencing abundant life in parent-child-educator-church relationships so that all involved can be strengthened through strategic partnerships with purpose. As partners, we must work together to ensure that our children are the best and brightest that they can be for the common good of all.

We live in a society where many people focus their attention on wanting to possess a better car, a bigger house, a higher paying job or even a spouse, and nothing is wrong with desiring any of those things, unless a person desires them only to make themselves look or feel better. We should not desire things at the expense of trying to discover self-esteem or creating a self-image to impress others. Some adults and children fall into this category.

Self-esteem is one of the most important possessions a person can have. It emerges from the very first contact a child has with his/her family. Even experiences in infancy lead to an awareness of self. As a child gets older, environmental experiences begin to shape his/her sense of self-concept and esteem. External stimuli such as rejection, negative attitudes, racial discrimination, and silent messages from others are learned, felt and impressed upon the psyche.

Examples of low self-esteem are seen too often in the faces of the following:

- Young female adolescents who want to get pregnant so they can love and be loved by their baby;
- Students who gravitate toward sitting in the back of the class because they are afraid of being called upon due to a lack of confidence or are ill-prepared to answer their teacher's questions;
- Young male adolescents who resort to gang violence because of their need to be accepted;
- Women whose main objective is to be married regardless of the person they marry;
- Those who are the perpetrators or victims of rape, incest and other forms of physical, verbal and emotional abuse;

- People who consciously try to alter their physical features to look like somebody else; and,
- Those who commit suicide.

What causes people to have low self-esteem? A survey conducted in 1950 by the University of Michigan and again in 1992 by Motivational Educational Entertainment, attributed the development of self-esteem in children to the following sources: (*Developing Positive Self-Images & Discipline in Black Children* by Jawanza Kunjufu):

1950	1992
1. home	1. peers
2. school	2. rap
3. church	3. television
4. peers	4. home
5. television	5. school

Imagine how the statistics changed as we entered a new millennium! If church wasn't even mentioned in 1992, and school was on the bottom of the list in ranking order of contributing sources of self-esteem, we certainly have our work cut out for us in 2010 and beyond.

My hope and prayer is that this book will serve as a resource for parents, teachers, and especially church leaders, to assemble a new paradigm of partnerships that will revolutionize us as a community so that we can no longer do business as usual as it relates to the holistic education of our children. If I could leave one legacy behind, it would be this: that every one of us would mentor another child in such a way that we would impart the best of ourselves and the brilliance of relevant information that is rightly applied, while stimulating their potential so the world would be better, brighter, and more beautiful because of our contribution to a deserving child who will, in return, do the same for the next generation. This is indeed the responsibility of parents, educators, and the Church as we work together under the adage: "It takes a village to raise a child."

The Philosophy of Education: Two Differing Views

THERE ARE NUMEROUS disturbing issues confronting America and the world; however, the montage of societal problems emanating from the nation's inner cities, particularly among urban, African-American youth, cannot be ignored. There must be a positive approach taken toward identifying and understanding the immediate needs of inner city dwellers and those living in the suburbs, as well as how the mission of educators and the Church (Christians who identify with the teachings and lifestyle of Jesus Christ), relate to these needs. Therefore, it is incumbent upon the faculty of our educational institutions and the members of the religious sector to move beyond the mere observance of problems plaguing the inner cities and surrounding communities, such as the disintegration of the family, homicide, genocide, declining values, illiteracy, promiscuity, drug and alcohol abuse, and gang violence. Parents, educators and Christians of all races and denominations must rise with a remedy that counteracts these negative conditions.

In lieu of accepting the pessimistic indicators of the media as the final word regarding the state of America's inner cities and periphery, we must promulgate a position of advocacy. This by no means suggests that we should be in support of that which destroys the fabric of cities within the United States and other nations—namely the immoral, self-destructive behavior that has caused many to shy away from urban areas altogether. We are not to become comfortable, middle-to-upper class suburbanites with little or no relevance to those in urban areas. Instead, it is the responsibility of parents in the home, educators in our schools and the Church to educate ourselves concerning the throes of society and to respond accordingly by instructing those charged to our stewardship in an excellent manner. Consequently, we should assume the role of evangelism as never before—that is, "the zealous preaching [teaching or educating] and dissemination of the gospel [the teachings of Jesus Christ], as through missionary work" (*The American Heritage Electronic Dictionary, Third Edition,* 1992). Thus, it becomes necessary to examine the philosophy and pedagogy of evangelism through Christian education and its influence upon mankind.

My Disclaimer

I must assert that not all secular education is bad or ungodly. My siblings and I were educated in the public school system, and our mother was an elementary school educator until she retired and my husband and I employed her, my two sisters and other qualified staff to teach in our church's Christian school. It has been my privilege to teach in both the public and private school sector, and to do so successfully. I have, however, anguished over the fact that many of the staples which I became accustomed to as a little girl such as praying in school (as led by the classroom teacher), and giving full attention to the authority figure in the classroom whether it be the teacher, substitute teacher or any other school employee, have been dishonored and dismantled. Due to a lack of respect for God and authority in general, optimal learning cannot take place. Many teachers find it difficult to manage their classrooms because of the unruly behavior of not just the students, but often times, the equally unruly behavior of some of their parents who have neglected the responsibility to nurture and discipline their children. Thus, there are a disproportionate number of students who slip through the cracks because of frustrated teachers, uninvolved parents, and a host of other problems that have caused some of our public schools to falter in the expectation of educating all of our students. It is not my intention to bash secular education, but rather, to define, contrast and compare it to that of Christian education which should begin in the home and extend to both the public and private sector as parents, educators and the Church agree to forge partnerships that will promote the mission of educating the whole child spiritually, intellectually, physically, and socially.

Secular Education Defined

Secular education is often steeped in a humanistic way of thinking as is evident through its rejection of Scriptural teaching. Emphasis may be placed upon existentialism and autonomy, stemming from the writings of Karl Marx before the *Communist Manifesto* (Baker, 1990). Consequently, this type of education promotes man as the "sole authority" while refuting the existence of God. Moreover, God's creation of the universe and mankind is replaced by Darwin's theory of evolution and Dewey's pragmatic views of education, as are taught within the American public school system.

According to a review of William Kilpatrick's book entitled *Why Johnny Can't Tell Right from Wrong*, the news from America's schools is disheartening. Kilpatrick cites three-million crimes committed on or near school property (16,000 per day), widespread drug and alcohol abuse, and sexual activity and teen pregnancy at an all-time high. The reason for such an alarming crisis is based upon the collapse of morality, and little to do with low academic achievement. Educational fads such as *values clarification* and the *dilemma method* have taken hold, where opinions as to *what is right for me* are thrown back and forth without dealing with the crux of the problem and offering solutions. Non-judgmental drug and sex education curriculums have been introduced which scarcely mention abstinence. Students are also encouraged to question the values of parents, the church, and other social establishments. Schools that have adapted this form of secular education have had disastrous results (Parker, 1994). Instead, the solution, Kilpatrick says, "is a return to character education: setting and enforcing standards of good behavior, giving students examples of good character from history and literature, and laying down solid rules and firm expectations" (Parker, *Book Satchel: Value-Neutral Education is No Solution*, 1994).

Perhaps a more concise definition of progressive education involves "the worship of science, a belief in the inherent goodness of man, the rejection of absolutes and fixed truth, the absence of genuine goals for education outside of the individual and his society, and sinister political implications" (Kenneth O. Gangel, 1983). Some say it is survival of society; others say it is the creation of an autonomous individual. Nevertheless, the objective of this type of education is the production of a particular kind of society. "Importance is not placed on the individual per se, but rather, on the group (or, in another version of this, on a new [or modern] 'man')" (Baker, *The Successful Christian*

School, 1990). Consequently, "man," in his unregenerate state, desires to express himself freely without moral or ethical restraint. The effects of this kind of behavior upon society, as a result, may be horrendous. However, there is an alternative view of education that is diametrically opposed to that of the secular domain as has been described thus far. It is this view that will be discussed in detail as a viable alternative to the trepidation of the progressive education movement—a view that serves as the antidote to the ills of society.

Christian Education Defined

The term "Christian" is defined as "a believer in Jesus as the Messiah prophesied in the Old Testament, or in the religion based on the teachings of Jesus; of or professing the religion based on His teachings; (and) having the qualities taught by Jesus Christ, as love, kindness, humility, etc" (*Webster's New World Dictionary*, 1990). Hence, the lifestyle of a Christian should reflect the principles outlined in the Bible, which is understood and accepted by those who profess such a lifestyle to be the infallible, authoritative word of God. Therefore, it is from this reliable source that Christian education is derived.

Education is "the knowledge or skill obtained or developed by a learning process" (*American Heritage Electronic Dictionary*, 1992). *Christian education*, however, is "the transmission of communication skills and the accumulated knowledge of society along with principles [especially moral] to individuals. This is more effectively done by teachers having authority to present material [that is a curriculum based upon the Bible] to students in order to motivate and stimulate the intellectual, as well as the spiritual appetite of the learner. Character is then developed by decisions made as principles are presented. Honest presentation causes there to be decisions made with the full assurance of knowing that there are consequences to either choice" (Baker, *The Successful Christian School*, 1990). Therefore, the mere process of conformity is not the objective, but rather, the process of transformation, which can only be accomplished through the work of the Holy Spirit. Thus, the autonomous man can literally become transformed by nature into a disciple of Jesus Christ through Christian education.

The words of Jesus Christ in John 13:35 state, "By this shall all men know that ye are my disciples, if ye have love one to another." The term *disciple* translated in the Greek text according to *Strong's Hebrew and Greek Dictionary*, is *mathetes*, which means "a learner, i.e., a pupil (or) disciple." A disciple then, is one who grasps, understands and applies the concepts taught by an instructor who has already mastered the subject material. In this respect, the instructor would be one whose life exemplifies the very character and nature of Jesus Christ. The culmination of Christianity, as a result, is not found in the Christian's mere confession of being a disciple of Jesus Christ. Instead, true discipleship is based upon the premise that one obeys the teaching of loving others as previously stated in the scriptural text. Consequently, evangelism through Christian education places emphasis upon the presentation of the gospel (or the teachings of Jesus Christ) through discipleship. Yet, the catalyst for sharing such a message is the compassion that the Church is to have for all men, in a social and moral sense, regardless of creed, ethnicity, or socioeconomic status. To love others then, involves the deliberate assent of the will as a matter of principle, duty and propriety. This is the impetus that leads to true discipleship of self and others.

A set of objectives has been associated with Christian education since the 1930's as introduced by Paul Vieth (Powers, 1981). According to Vieth, these objectives are:

1. To foster in growing persons a consciousness of God as a reality in human experience, and a sense of personal relationship to Him.

2. To develop in growing persons such an understanding and appreciation of the personality, life, and teachings of Jesus as will lead to experiencing Him as Savior and Lord, loyalty to Him and His cause, and manifest itself in daily life and conduct.

3. To foster in growing persons as progressive and continuous development of Christ-like character.

4. To develop in growing persons the ability and disposition to participate in and contribute constructively in the building of a social order throughout the world, embodying the ideal of the Fatherhood of God and the brotherhood of man.

5. To develop in growing persons the ability and disposition to participate in the organized society of Christians – the Church.

6. To develop in growing persons an appreciation of the meaning and importance of the Christian

family, and the ability and disposition to participate in and contribute constructively to the life of this primary social group.

7. To lead growing persons into a Christian interpretation of life and the universe; the ability to see in it God's purpose and plan; and a life philosophy built on this interpretation.

8. To effect in growing persons the assimilation of the best religious experience of the race, preeminently that which is recorded in the Bible, as an effective guidance to present experience. (Powers, *Christian Education Handbook: Resources for Church Leaders*, 1981)

The philosophy of Christian education is in direct contrast to that of secular education. Emphasis is placed upon the development of character and the intellect. The lifestyle of the instructor, as well as the student, plays a substantial role in the teaching and learning process. Curriculum content based upon Biblical precepts is essential, while the work of the Holy Spirit in the life of the student is equally important. Conformity to a belief system is not the objective of the Christian educator. Rather, it is the transformation that takes place as a matter of the pupil's will to understand, accept, and apply the knowledge presented by the teacher. Hence, the educator, the pupil, the Holy Spirit, and a Biblically-based curriculum, become the components for a successful philosophy and pedagogy of Christian education.

Christian education is most effective when it is introduced in the home beginning with the parent-child relationship. Values taught early on should be those reflected by the parent(s) or legal guardian(s) whose life and lifestyle are guided by biblical principles inherent to modeling and teaching excellence in character, training, discipline, academics, and service. In that regard, Christian education can also take place in a secular school given the notion that Christian parents and teachers partner together to reinforce what is to be learned and valued both at home and within the walls of our educational institutions.

Demographic Trends and Urban, African-American Dilemmas

THE INNER CITY is the central portion of a city, comprising its business district and the areas of housing and industry that immediately surround it. There is a resurgence of unsublimated power that lies within this area, particularly amongst the African-American community. Hopelessness, despair, and stereotypical phraseology, have plagued many—from the conflagration of the Civil Rights Movement, to issues which are still prevalent in today's society. However, there is a new clarion call specifically made to the Church—that is, the importance of evangelizing the inner city.

In the 19th century, the inner cities of the United States were dynamic and growing, fueled by the expansion of business and industry, along with the influx of immigrants. In the mid 20th century, however, cities began losing their white, middle-class populations to the suburbs. As the construction of new highways made large-scale automobile commuting feasible, government programs (such as federally guaranteed home mortgages for World War II veterans), encouraged suburban home construction. Major inner-city stores followed their customers by relocating to suburban area shopping malls. The population remaining in the inner cities thereafter was largely comprised of African-Americans, Hispanics, and immigrants, and the industrial jobs that supported this population disappeared as the factories were closed or relocated (*The Inner City*, 1995).

Federally funded urban renewal programs and efforts aimed at rescuing abandoned housing have been used in the attempt to reverse the condition of the inner city. Even so, the movement toward gentrification of some areas by middle-class professionals has rarely reached the areas in greatest need. In fact, housing shortages are sometimes exacerbated by this redevelopment as poorer residents are forced to move from areas they can no longer afford. Consequently, many urban planners feel that "without massive employment programs and fundamental and innovative improvements in mass transit and other facilities, the inner cities will remain conspicuous areas of decay" (*The 1995 Grolier Multimedia Encyclopedia*, 1995).

Demographic Trends

The population of the United States, as well as that of the world, has been growing rapidly. In fact, it was estimated that 42.1% of the total United States population would reside in cities with 750,000 or more inhabitants by the year 2000 (*Electronic Arts 3D Atlas 1.1 Macintosh CD—United States Urbanization*, 1994). Additionally, the total number of urban dwellers in cities with inhabitants of 750,000 and above was projected to reach approximately 115,900,000 by the year 2000, thereby causing the United States to be ranked as second (with China ranking first and India, third) among countries with significant urban populations (*Electronic Arts 3D Atlas 1.1 Macintosh CD—United States Urbanization—Total Persons in Big Cities*, 1994). Hence, an awesome task of evangelism lies ahead for the Church, particularly as we move forward into a time when minorities will soon become the majority population in our nation. Please notice the following:

> Further examination of United States population figures reveals a changing ethnic composition. Caucasians still are a majority in the population, though a shrinking one. Blacks represent the second largest group, followed by Asians, who have increased in percentage in recent years. American Indians are only a small fraction of that population.
>
> These changes have urgent implications for the Christian educator. The first challenge to the thinking of churches and educators is the rapidly increasing world population—and the decreasing percentage of that population living in the United States. It presents a clarion call for cross-cultural education that cannot be ignored for another generation without serious erosion to the influence of the church worldwide.
>
> But cross-cultural communication is not a matter for overseas missions alone. Although Asians, blacks, and other groups are yet a minority in the United States, these groups are increasing in number and as a percentage of the total population. Churches in every metropolitan center in the United States must seek ways to teach the Word of God to those who may be first generation citizens and who may not fit into the typical white, Anglo-Saxon, middle class congregation. Christians must be educated to be more concerned—not only about the world, but about those of other cultures who may or may not live or work where they do. (Eleanor Daniel, 1987)

American Christians must become aware of the shift

in population and the racial composition of their homeland. The Great Commission of Jesus to His disciples according to Matthew 28:19-20 states: "Go ye therefore, and teach all nations, baptizing them in the name of the Father, and of the Son, and of the Holy Ghost: Teaching them to observe all things whatsoever I have commanded you: and lo, I am with you always, even unto the end of the world." Thus, the mandate for the Church is to make disciples of all nations (or peoples), regardless of their ethnicity or socioeconomic status. But how can one effectively evangelize the population of the other nations if the hopeless and helpless, especially among our children, remain within one's own reach? Jesus Christ Himself answers this thought-provoking question in Acts 1:8 by saying, "…ye shall be witnesses unto me both in Jerusalem, and in all Judaea, and in all Samaria, and unto the uttermost part of the earth." Herein is a concept which should be immediately acknowledged and utilized by the Christian both at home, at church, and within our school systems. One's immediate community (or "Jerusalem") should be given priority, as it becomes the first missionary field.

Urban, African-American Dilemmas

Contrary to popular belief and the media, many inner cities are comprised of racial groups outside of the African-American culture as well, such as Hispanics and Asians. In fact, growing numbers of poor white Americans may be forming a new underclass: a generation of young unwed mothers on the public dole (which seems to be a portrait of inner-city Baltimore) (Bogert, 1994). Additionally, whites below the poverty line are more widely scattered throughout Baltimore than blacks, who can still find it extremely difficult to move into a white neighborhood. Even so, according to a study conducted by Susan Weiner at the Urban Institute in Washington, DC, "poor black people are seven times more likely to live in a poor neighborhood than poor white people are" (Bogert C., 1994). Still, other problems pervade the inner cities, especially those cited amongst African-Americans.

Parents, educators, and the Church must collectively acknowledge that the urban community is facing a crisis that, if not dealt with, may escalate into conditions of rage similar to the riots that occurred in South Central Los Angeles, California. Even though we have achieved the unimaginable precedent of electing our first African-American, Barack Obama, as President of our nation and the leader of the free world in 2008, racial unrest among African-Americans still exists due to prejudices, inequality, economic injustice and police insensitivity as evidenced in the treatment of some blacks via the media.

Research has proven that African-American death rates are higher than any other racial-ethnic group with regard to infant mortality rates, cancer, diabetes, strokes, heart disease and HIV/AIDS. High school dropout rates, unemployment, children born out of wedlock, murder and a myriad of other incorrigible statistics plague our African-American men and women as well. In addition, traditional roles of husband and wife within the family have changed with the economic and social demands of society. Biblically based, family values have been exchanged for selfish ambitions resulting in a flagrant disregard for morality. Thus, the disintegration of the family has led to a perpetual cycle of welfare dependency due to the lack of fathers in the home.

The effects upon the family unit within the African-

American culture were and are disproportionate when compared to that of white America. Consider the following statistics concerning single parent families as reported by the United States Census Bureau:

- Between 1980 and 1994, the proportion of all black families that were headed by single parents climbed from 52% to 65%. By 2000, however, this percentage had declined slightly to 63.2%. Among both white and Hispanic families, the percentage maintained by single parents increased between 1980 and 2000, among whites from 17.1% in 1980 to 26% in 2000, and from 25.9% to 35.4% for Hispanics. However, these increases still left the percentage of black families maintained by single parents more than twice the percentage for white families, and 75% higher than that for Hispanics.
- The fraction of single-parent families maintained by men is steadily increasing. Nevertheless, in 2000 the overwhelming majority of black single-parent families (90.1%) were maintained by women, and so were 79.3% of white single-parent families.
- In 2000, 19.2 million children under 18 lived with one parent, including about 58.2% of all black children and 23% of all white children. In 1998, for both black and non-Hispanic white households, the average number of children per household living with single fathers was 2.0. The average number of children in the families of black single mothers (2.5) and white single mothers (2.2) was higher, as was the average number of children in two-parent black (2.6) and white

(2.4) families.

David Blankenhorn, author of *Fatherless America* (1995), stated that "the culture change from stable, two-parent homes to the father's abandonment of his responsibilities of marriage and parenting is America's most urgent social problem" (Walter G. Fremont, 1995). This sentiment must be profoundly echoed by the entire religious community as it seeks to examine the social effects of this pervading dilemma upon our society.

The lack of positive male role models in the home has led many young people down a pathway of self-destruction. Youth have sought acceptance in inner city gangs (which could in a sense be viewed as "surrogate families"), in search of love, identification, and approval. In fact, the vast majority of juveniles in detention centers and reformatories and violent criminals in America's penal system are children of fatherless homes.

Another dilemma facing the urban, African-American community and the nation as a whole is the rampant use of guns which are easily made available either at home or "on the street." Many acts of violence take place as a result of the nation's youth becoming involved in the drug culture with its deceptive lure of fame and fortune.

The declining morals evident in America's public schools have caused many African-American parents to reconsider having their children educated in the system unless there are major reforms made. In fact, when Linda Schrenko served as the head of Georgia's public education system, she stated the following:

"African-American parents with children in inner-city districts have been among the strongest supporters of charter schools—campuses free of typical school regulations—and vouchers, which allow parents to send their children to private schools. Even the buildings in inner-city schools tend to be rundown. What they [parents] are saying is they are tired of schools that are violent. They're tired of it, and they want the best for their kids, like anybody else" (Salzer, 1999).

Privatization (the management of public schools by private companies), is a popular topic of discussion among many parents. A study conducted by Research Atlanta surveyed over 700 Georgia parents to find that more than 50% of all African-American parents with children in the public school system are in favor of privatization. About 33% of white parents supported the same idea. Ben Scafidi, co-author of this study and assistant professor in the Andrew Young School of Policy Studies at Georgia State University, concludes that "groups for whom public schools don't seem to work well are most open to new ideas" (Salzer, *Faith in Public Schools Fades: Growing Support for Privatization*, 1999).

Another current debate in both political and educational circles is the idea of school choice. Many would agree that this issue along with the acceptance or rejection of vouchers is a major dividing line between Democrats and Republicans, as well as between whites and blacks. Although this may very well be a hot political topic, it is not an exclusively racist or elitist issue. Parents and educators alike who desire for their students to achieve success are advocates for excellence and accountability, and the best option for attaining such is removing students from underperforming schools and placing them in institutions where they can excel and compete globally. One study after another proves that there is a demand for something new and different, thus the need for educational reform is greater than ever. Many parents desire vouchers so that they can choose to send their children to schools that offer academic excellence and accountability. A national poll released by the Joint Center for Political and Economic Studies found a trend toward growing support of tuition vouchers, particularly among African-American parents. As a result, there will be an influx of students from urban, inner-city communities enrolling in private and parochial schools. Programs such as the Children's Scholarship Fund, funded by Wal-Mart heir, John Walton, and financier Ted Forstmann, serve as proof that there is a tremendous ground swell of support for school choice. Under this program alone, the parents of over 1.25 million children across the country applied for partial scholarships to help their children attend private and parochial schools (Schmoke, *Why School Vouchers Can Help Inner-City Children*, 1999).

In terms of Christian education, the Church has yet to have reached the black community with any degree of success (Eleanor Daniel J. W., 1987). It can be concluded then, after examining the dilemmas within America's inner cities as well as the political and educational views of many African-American parents that an epidemic exists. Illiteracy, violence and immorality are prevalent, leaving countless youth and adults seemingly disenfranchised. Christians who recognize the severity of this malady must rise with conviction and solutions to combat the ills that plague our society. The words of Victor Hugo echo this sentiment: "Greater than the tread of mighty armies, is an idea whose time has come."

With this heart-felt persuasion, the Church can evangelize those areas presently being forsaken by the overwhelming majority by embracing the idea of providing an alternative to the public school system as a matter of conviction as well as choice.

A Parent's Mentoring Mandate

*Every generation finds it hard to hear what its children need
—because its childhood is still ringing in its ears.*
—Ellen Goodman

I CAN REMEMBER growing up playing games like Dodge Ball, Mother May I, Hopscotch, Hide and Go Seek, Jacks, and so on. There was a time when everyone played outside until the street lights came on, at which time I could hear my mother (or somebody else's mother) shouting that it was time to come in the house. If we did anything wrong such as speaking disrespectfully, hanging out with the wrong crowd, or going somewhere we weren't supposed to go and someone found out about it, we would get in trouble with our parents, guardians, neighbors and anyone else who had a stake in our childhood development. Everybody helped to rear everyone else's children, because that's the way it was. But times have changed!

Now we live in a technologically advanced era where the information highway has replaced the bridge of building relationships. Instead, we are confronted daily with emails, instant messages and access to Facebook, Twitter and MySpace via access to the internet on our computers and cell phones, with text messaging and other high tech capabilities; PDAs; GPS systems; MP3 players; iPods; cable TV; and video games designed to stimulate this sight and sound generation. Electronic gadgets of all kinds come in a variety of shapes, sizes and colors with the purpose of introducing messages from the media to the minds of adults and children alike. How many parents and children are guilty of spending more time at home with televisions, computers, cell phones and iPods rather than with each other? John Milton has been quoted as saying, "*Hypocrisy [is] the only evil that walks invisible.*" This statement simply underscores the fact that we're all guilty to some extent.

Some things change for the better and others for the worse. What we must determine is what needs to change in and around us so that we prepare this and the next generation to excel holistically. In order for this to occur we must know that there are biblical principles by which parents can mentor and thus adequately prepare our children to achieve greatness, and it all begins within the home.

Mentoring Principles to Live By

> *1. We must practice what we preach.* Our children are wise enough to learn from and follow our actions because they speak much louder than our words. (For example, how can we expect our children to attend church regularly when we show up when we want to? How can we demand that they save money and spend wisely if we can't properly manage our own finances? How can we lecture them about bringing good grades home and being an excellent student when we are slothful and mediocre both at work and at home?)

I Corinthians 9:27 (New King James Version): *But I discipline my body and bring it into subjection, lest, when I have preached to others, I myself should become disqualified.*

2. **We must be consistent in providing discipline and instruction.** Don't lay down a law with a child that you are not prepared to enforce! *(Episodes of the television show "Super Nanny" can attest to that, to which she would even say "Amen!")* Discipline strengthens and provides structure for children. Setting rules for them to obey is absolutely necessary in helping to instill confidence, self-control, self-respect as well as a healthy respect for authority. Establishing rules helps to prepare our children for the reality of coping with and succeeding in the world. But if we are not consistent in setting boundaries and structure, what we actually teach them is that rules don't really matter and that they can do whatever they want.

Proverbs 10:28 (Message Bible): *The road to life is a disciplined life; ignore correction and you're lost for good.*

3. **Use every opportunity to pass on important values and life lessons.** Each new day provides another opportunity to teach, listen to, and learn from our children. We need to acquaint ourselves with them by knowing where they're going, what they're

doing, why they're doing it, and who they're doing it with! If they're in our house and are being supported by us financially, then they're still our responsibility, regardless of their age. Age is just a number, and the number eighteen does not mean that they have entered into the age of independence and maturity (even though their physical appearance may say otherwise). Maturity is a process that happens as a result of wisdom (learning life's lessons and applying what is learned in the right context).

Deuteronomy 4:9 (New King James Version): *Only take heed to yourself, and diligently keep yourself, lest you forget the things your eyes have seen, and lest they depart from your heart all the days of your life. And* **teach them** *to your children and your grandchildren.*

Deuteronomy 6:6-9 (Amplified Bible): *And these words which I am commanding you this day shall be [first] in your [own] minds and hearts; [then] You shall whet and sharpen them so as to make them penetrate, and teach and impress them diligently upon the [minds and] hearts of your children, and shall talk of them when you sit in your house and when you walk by the way, and when you lie down and when you rise up. And you shall bind them as a sign upon your hand, and they shall be as frontlets (forehead bands) between your eyes. And you shall write them upon the doorposts of your house and* *on your gates.*

What is it that we are to teach them?

- ***Teach them to love and obey God's Word.*** Church attendance is a good start, but it's not enough. Those we mentor must see us enthusiastically serving God with prayer, Bible study and service to others so that they'll desire to do the same. Even if they stray, they'll come back to what they've been taught. ***Proverbs 22:6*** says: *"Train up a child in the way he should go: and when he is old, he will not depart from it."*

- ***Teach them to fear God. Psalm 34:11 (KJV)*** says, *"Come, ye children, hearken unto me: I will teach you the fear of the LORD."* Fear in this sense is defined as moral reverence. When parents teach children to reverence and respect God because it is right or righteous, it becomes easier for children to respect their parents, teachers and other authority figures.

- ***Teach them how to have fun, be happy, and help others by setting the example before them.*** Uptight, stressed out, selfish parents will produce uptight, stressed out, selfish children! Life is not about us, but about those who are influenced and blessed by and through us.

- *Teach them how to have a strong work ethic.* Once a child begins to walk, he or she can be taught to become responsible. Chores should be given that are age-appropriate and rewarded, while other responsibilities should be given to show that it is better to give (of one's time, talents and treasures), than it is to receive as the Bible declares.

- *Teach them to have a love for learning during each stage of their development.* From the cute and cuddly stage of infancy to the active toddler stage, to the show and tell school years, to the teenage years (when the process of separation begins as a result of them wanting to spend more times with their friends and less time with their parents), to young adulthood, we must strive to: play with them; teach them new things; listen to them; get to know them and their friends; spend quality time with them; share stories and experiences; trust them; and most importantly, love them unconditionally and lavishly. Developing a love for learning will cause our children to thrive and not just survive.

What must we learn ourselves?

- *Assume the best, but brace ourselves for the worst, especially once we learn the facts.* Even though we know our children better than anyone else and want to take up for them, we must not sacrifice the success of their future by refusing to believe and accept the truth about wrong choices they've made. Even the best of children misbehave, because no one is perfect, including church folk, PK's (preacher's kids) and their families. Unacceptable behavior and conversations must be nipped in the bud!

- ***Learn from our mistakes so that our children do not repeat them.*** We shouldn't live in the past, but we should learn from the past so that our present and our children's future are not held captive by it.

Mentoring the children God has assigned to us as parents is critical if they are to inherit a spiritual legacy and serve as leaders in their own right. We must think generationally and realize that we must prepare our children to take our place in positions of leadership and influence in the church and in every arena in our society as well as in global markets. Jesus said it best in John 15:8 (King James Version) by saying, *"Herein is My Father glorified, that ye bear much fruit; so shall ye be My disciples* (pupils, learners)." Although it is necessary for us to focus on our career paths and issues that are important to us, let us not forget to spend the necessary time and energy in ensuring that the health and well-being of the family is a priority that will not be compromised. When God is glorified in our personal lives and in all of our relationships, then the next generation will be prepared to fulfill their destiny.

More Parent-Child Strategies

Defining a Generation

THOSE WHO WERE born during the eras of depression and war between 1925 and 1942 were known as the *Silent Generation*. After World War II, there was a major increase in the number of births as the times led to more economic prosperity. This period of time, between the years of 1946 and 1964, gave birth to the *Baby Boomer Generation*, the group who currently controls the majority of our country's industrial, political, and economic prosperity. The *Silent Generation* operated by the motto "Get it done," while the *Baby Boomers* were no strangers to hard work because of the example set by their parents. As a result, many *Boomers* determined to become financially independent and materialistically driven.

Generation X was the generation that followed the *Baby Boomers*. Born between 1965 and 1980, they were reared while watching television, playing Atari 2600 video games and were introduced to a whole new world through personal computers. They were reared in the 1970s and 1980s and saw this country undergo a shift to a more individualistic phase and focus. The media has described this generation as "underemployed, overeducated, intensely private and unpredictable."

Following *Generation X* is what is known as *Generation Y*—a generation that rivals the *Baby Boomers* in size—and will soon rival them economically. These are the sons and daughters of *Boomers* and *Xers*. Born between 1979 and 1994, they are more than 60 million strong and three times the size of *Generation X* according to an internet source. Also known as the *Millennium Generation*, they are the largest group to be born since the *Boomers*.

Those who desire to reach *Generation Y* must learn to think like them because they differ greater from the generations that preceded them. *Generation Y* is more racially diverse, politically correct, behaviorally tolerant and religiously intolerant than their predecessors. They have been born in the era of postmodernism which has implications across the spectrum in regard to their beliefs and how they relate to others.

What does all this mean?

In essence, we as parents must actively pursue fostering a relationship with our children by learning how to communicate with, listen to, and instruct them by using methods that are both principle-centered and generationally-appropriate. Thus, the need for sharing strategies that are conducive to establishing healthy parent-child relationships is warranted. The following strategies are those that my husband and I have both learned and applied in the rearing of our children, many of which are founded on biblical principles. Another excellent resource is Steven Covey's book entitled *The Seven Habits of Highly Effective Families*.

Strategy #1: We must pray for our children daily. I realized early on that prayer really does change not only things, but most importantly, people. My husband and I grew up in Christian homes that were the impetus for our desire to maintain a relationship with God and to model it before our children. Such a relationship began with and is sustained by prayer, and it extended to the way we decided to rear our children. We prayed for God's protection and provision regarding their spiritual, intellectual, emotional, physical and social growth and development, and we still do although they are now young adults. I can remember explicitly praying for everything I could think of concerning them from the womb through their formative years and so on. I would dedicate one focus per month throughout the course of an entire year to pray for each of my children in areas regarding their personalities, behavior, natural and developed gifts, acquaintances, close friends and the mates that they would one day marry. Believe it or not, I even prayed that they would be caught if they behaved in an inappropriate manner so that they would learn to accept the consequences of their choices and that we, as their parents, would learn not to turn a blind eye and a deaf ear to their wrongdoing. And most importantly, I prayed that each of my children would come to know and serve God as a personal decision that they would make.

"All your children *shall be* taught by the Lord, And great *shall be* the peace of your children. In righteousness you shall be established; You shall be far from oppression, for you shall not fear; And from terror, for it shall not come near you."
—Isaiah 54:13-14 (NKJV)

Strategy #2: Realize that each child was created by God for a purpose and that it is our responsibility as parents to help them find it. Every one of us is as unique in design, personality and abilities as our fingerprints. God did not create us to exist merely to take up time and space, but to enjoy the journey of learning, growing and understanding ourselves and what we can achieve. It is the parents' responsibility to create an insatiable desire within his/her child for exploring the wondrous capabilities of the mind, body, and spirit in ways that are aligned with God's masterful plan for their lives. Therefore, we are to watch for opportunities that give us insight into the ways that our children excel in academics, sports, extra-curricular activities, interpersonal relationships and other activities at home, church, school, and in other arenas that attract their attention and develop their passions. We are not to push them into, but rather to gently direct them towards what will fulfill them as unique individuals who can contribute positively to the world around them.

Jeremiah 29:11 (MSG): I know what I'm doing. I have it all planned out—plans to take care of you, not abandon you, plans to give you the future you hope for.

Strategy #3: Proper nurturing involves encouragement, instruction, and correction. Too many parents err on the side of caution in rearing their children with the notion that they do not want to risk disciplining them and not befriending them. Let me go on record as saying that a parent should not desire to be their child's best friend.

Rather, parents are to be the first authority figure in the home that their child learns to love, respect, and obey. Children then are to be encouraged and instructed to do what is morally and ethically right, but not at the expense of never being corrected and given consequences for making unwise choices. Godly instruction involves training in righteousness, that is to say, in a lifestyle that most resembles right behavior. Children then are taught that right and wrong, good and evil, do exist, and that the choice is theirs to make with direction given by their parents and other respected authority figures. The threefold cord of encouragement for right behavior, instruction in life's lessons, and correction when wrong choices are made, is biblically sound and thus provides a proper nurturing environment for any child.

Ephesians 6:1-3 (NKJV): *Children, obey your parents in the Lord, for this is right. "Honor your father and mother," which is the first commandment with promise: "that it may be well with you and you may live long on the earth."*

Strategy #4: Effective communication is a tool that will help to build and maintain healthy parent-child relationships. The parents must first agree to communicate openly and honestly their expectations in rearing children so that both husband and wife (in a two-parent home) are on the same page. Husbands and wives who fail to communicate properly with each other will send mixed signals to their children, which can be used against them as the children grow older and wiser. Parents then must seek to communicate better with each other and to establish healthy channels of communication at each stage of a child's development through empathic listening, clear verbal language, and non-verbal cues. Empathic listening requires parents to place themselves in the place of the child to understand their feelings and point of view. As children grow older, they can indeed pattern themselves in the same regard to be empathic in their listening and communication skills. Here are other important communication strategies to consider as adapted from *The Seven Habits of Highly Effective Families* by Steven Covey:

- *Build an emotional bank account. (View every problem as an opportunity to make a deposit. Each problem is asking for a response, not a reaction. Be kind, apologize and forgive often, be loyal to those not present, and keep your promises.)*
- *The way you treat any relationship in the family will eventually affect every relationship in the family.*
- *Seek to understand rather than to judge in order to have influence.*
- *Use "I" messages which are more horizontal rather than "You" messages which are more vertical (indicating that one person is better or of more worth than the other).*
- *The key to your family culture is how you treat the child that tests you the most.*
- *Healthy spouse-to-spouse and parent/child relationships guard against the **four cancers** that are detrimental to the synergy of family life: **criticizing, complaining, comparing** and **competing.***

James 1:19 (NKJV): *So then, my beloved brethren, let every* *man be swift to hear, slow to speak, slow to wrath.*

Strategy #5: Intentionally schedule time for teaching/learning opportunities. Parents should make every effort to set aside time for children to learn and appreciate faith, family values, and traditions as well as history, cultural diversity, and other opportunities for enlightenment. Family activities could include church attendance and participation, vacations, mission trips, museum visits, historical sites, theatrical productions, musical concerts, and other creative planning for the purpose of exposing children to different people, places, and things.

Proverbs 9:9 (NKJV): *Give instruction to a wise man, and he will be still wiser; Teach a just man, and he will increase in learning.*

Remember that relationships in the family require constant attention because the expectation of being emotionally nurtured and supported is constant. We get into trouble when we take our loved ones for granted and treat a stranger at the door better than those who are closest and dearest to us. Instead of taking our spouses and children for granted, we must make a conscious, constant effort to apologize, ask for forgiveness, express love and appreciation, and value each other. It is our responsibility to love and care enough not to avoid confrontation, but to address issues proactively in ways that are positive and respectful so that issues are solved rather than ignored. When issues of any kind are left unchecked, they can cause the dissolution and estrangement of many family relationships.

5
Partnering with Public and Private School Educators

KURT L. SCHMOKE, FORMER Mayor of the City of Baltimore, announced that he was a proponent for school choice and vouchers at a Manhattan Institute luncheon in New York. As a Democrat and an African-American mayor, he was considered a maverick by his fellow party colleagues for expressing such an idea. However, Schmoke spoke candidly on behalf of many parents, particularly those in the urban community:

> Why school choice? Two reasons: excellence and accountability. Parents want academic excellence for their children. They also want to know that there is someone in their child's school who is accountable for achieving those high academic standards. Under a school choice plan, a parent would have options. There would be consequences for a school's poor performance. Parents could pull their children out of poorly performing schools and enroll them some place else. If exercising this option leads to a mass exodus from certain underachieving schools, schools will learn this painful lesson: schools will either improve or close due to declining enrollments.
>   Some say that school choice, especially vouchers, will weaken public education. My response

is that choice can only strengthen public education by introducing competition and accountability into the mix. Others claim that school choice is undemocratic. My response to them is that choice is in keeping with the aspirations for freedom that framed the core of American democracy. As former Delaware governor Pete Du Pont once wrote, "It's about the liberty to choose what's best for your children." All of us should have that choice.

Some say that school choice is elitist, or even racist. The truth is that black low-income children are among the prime victims of the nation's failing public schools. African-American parents know this all too well. This is why they have been so open to the idea of school choice (Schmoke, K. L., 1999).

The values of Christian education are to be established first in the home. Morehouse President and author, Dr. Robert M. Franklin, asserts that "As children move from homes that are ethical learning centers into the schools, we must insist that schools also engage in nurturing moral character" (Franklin, 2007). In order for students to thrive outside of the home environment, parents must actively pursue relationships of accountability with educators in both public and private schools. This means that standards must be raised so that no child is left behind because of inferior, inadequate resources or disinterested, disengaged parents and teachers. We must require a higher caliber of faculty and a curriculum that challenges our children and prepares them to compete with the best and brightest across the globe. Every student must be presented with opportunities to excel in ways that will engage their respective learning propensities as a variety of teaching methods are utilized. Excellence, effectiveness, and efficiency are to be demanded in staff, state of the art facilities, technologies and programs that encourage student success across the spectrum of all core competencies and extra-curricular activities.

I am aware that much of what happens in our educational system in regard to reform is a matter of political persuasion. However, after seeing what was accomplished through the grass roots effort of a community organizer who became the first elected African-American President of our nation, I am certain that parents and educators can form community partnerships that can effect change for the better in our public and private school systems for the sake of our children.

There are a number of ways in which these partnerships between parents and educators in the public and private sector can be established, beginning with an initial conversation of interest and intent. By this, I mean that parents or educators can take the initiative to meet face-to-face to express their concern for the welfare of the student to ensure his or her academic success along with the continual development of character training based on values and expectations espoused by both parties. This joint venture then moves beyond the initial conversation and takes on a life that endures throughout the school year. Principals and other resource teachers instrumental to the growth of the child should also be sought out so that the support system grows larger and stronger, thereby making the pathway toward a common goal believable and achievable by all involved.

I cannot overemphasize the necessity of volunteerism,

which helps students to see and know for certain that their parents are willingly involved in their educational pursuits, and is essential in creating meaningful relationships with classroom teachers and school administrators to ensure present and future academic growth. Parents and educators can also work together to raise funds to enhance the quality of education, especially in private schools that do not have access to government or state funding. As we realize that we have a primary stake in the learning processes of our students, then we will take ownership of the very schools and programs in which our students are enrolled and where educators are there not merely for a pay check (that needs to be commensurate with their skills and talents), but because they have a zealous passion for teaching. And if high standards are not met, then we have the option to choose to remove our students and place them in a school where they can flourish in every respect, for that is their right and our choice as their parents.

The Role of an Educator

The epitome of teaching involves getting students immersed in a lesson that causes them to be engaged and in touch with both the teacher and his or her fellow students. This challenging task involves much more than the attitude of the teacher; the method of teaching itself is equally important. One may choose the lecture method, allowing for student reflection and individual study, while another instructor prefers a more interactive approach such as group discussions and cooperative learning opportunities. Whatever the methodology, the instructor must ensure that the lesson is interesting, and that it comes across in a manner that causes the student to be intellectually captivated so that the subject matter is comprehended and applied within the right context.

An educator must strive to be an effective communicator in the areas of speaking, listening and writing. Three specific areas of fluency regarding text, people, and schedule, must continue to be cultivated and refined. Textual fluency involves knowing the subject matter well enough to leave an indelible mark upon the student. The teacher must then understand the people to be taught in order to know how to reach them individually. It is also imperative that the teacher understands his or her own style of learning. Schedule fluency addresses the area of time management as it relates to lesson preparation and presentation (*Mastering Teaching*, 1991).

Although there is no higher call on earth than to teach in my opinion, the reality of teaching involves the giving of oneself to the task. Methods of communicating what is to be taught must change with the times. Advances in technology with access to a wealth of information on the internet can indeed enhance the teaching/learning process for both the educator and student. Just as the means of communicating a message must vary, so does the presentation of the teacher's lesson. The instructor must realize that all students learn differently. The age as well as the learning style of the audience should be considered in the preparation stage. Therefore, the teacher must grasp an understanding of the diversity of learning styles in order to be more productive in his or her approach to teaching.

There are four basic learning styles: auditory, visual,

kinesthetic, and tactile. An instructor's teaching must be geared in some way to reach the learning styles of the students. As a result, the teacher must be creative concerning the strategies used in order to get the subject matter across to the students. A variety of methods can be used by the teacher in order to communicate the lesson to the student effectively. The auditory learner will respond more readily to the lecture method, memorization and recall. Those who are visually stimulated learn best when the teacher uses PowerPoints, overheads, posters, cue cards, videos, and handouts of classroom information. Kinesthetic learners appreciate subject matter set to music, or any learning that involves bodily movement. Tactile teaching, however, is geared toward the student who enjoys working with clay, manipulative objects, and writing. Illustrations and real life situations should be used to enhance the lesson. The teacher must ask questions and seek answers according to these learning styles.

    One of the objectives of every teacher should be to build self-esteem or confidence in the life of students. This begins to surface as the teacher consistently affirms the student publicly and privately, thereby acknowledging the fact that there is untapped and unlimited potential waiting to be released. Unless the teacher makes a demand on the student's latent ability, it will remain undiscovered and unused. In fact, the instructors who go the extra mile by investing necessary time and energy into their students are the ones who are remembered for years to come. It is no wonder why persons who later become successful in life can look back and give credit to those who made them work harder. These teachers left an indelible mark upon those who had the privilege of benefiting from their tutelage.

It has been said that teachers need to be students of what they teach and of what their listeners need to learn. This is especially true in regards to determining how to teach a certain subject. The method to be used is determined by the ages, learning styles, and specific needs of the targeted audience. For instance, a child who may be diagnosed as having Attention Deficit Hyperactivity Disorder (ADHD) needs to have the lesson presented in a lively format with time allotted for a physical activity to reinforce concepts taught. This student may need the teacher's undivided attention, while another student seems to be self-motivated and as a result, needs very little help from the classroom teacher to excel. The educator's approach to teaching, whether they teach in a public or private school, must be geared toward the needs of the students as well as their capacity or level of learning. And it is the parents' responsibility, as well as the role of school administration, to ensure that this kind of teaching and learning is in effect and is monitored consistently.

The Responsibility of the Church

THE CHURCH, TYPICALLY known as "the Body of Christ," is to serve in a subjective role—that is, the Church (or the subject) is to point others to God (the object). Christians are called to do the will of God in effectively delivering the love and Word of God to the world. This task of proclaiming God's commandments to those who do not know the Christ of the gospel is evangelism. Consequently, the Church must evangelize domestically (as well as globally) by planting seeds of salvation, social justice, physical healing, and wholeness into the fallow ground of urban, suburban, and rural America. This prodigious mission involves the acknowledgment of dilemmas that primarily plague today's society, as well as the provision of strategies to bring restoration, healing, and hope from a biblical perspective. Therefore, Christians must sense a mandate to immediately counteract the negative influences that exist by actively and aggressively pursuing the work of rebuilding families and communities presently in disarray. The African-American community is in need of such an investment.

In order to receive a clear vision of the Church's responsibility, there must be a search for truth through the lens of "history" (or the past efforts of Christendom and the tragic failures of institutionalism); "contemporary culture" (which provides understanding of today's world and implications for the Church's ministry in it); and "scripture" (which sets forth the nature of the church, its mission in the world, and basic principles governing the essential tasks of the church's mission) (Eleanor Daniel J. W., 1987). These three lenses, as suggested by Gene Getz, will correct the blurred vision of the present Church's ministry. Furthermore, Getz concludes:

> Once we develop a proper perspective biblically, historically, and culturally, we must develop a contemporary strategy based particularly on New Testament principles; we must determine current needs in our own local church, formulate relevant objectives and goals, devise contemporary forms and structures, and use every legitimate resource to be a New Testament church in contemporary culture (Getz, 1974).

This three-lens vantage point clearly demonstrates how the church can effectively utilize evangelism through Christian education. First, there must be an effort made to research what the church's mission was from a historical perspective. Second, persons within the Church must determine to relate the historic purpose of the Church with its mission in the present. Last, there must be an analysis of how the Church can fulfill the Great Commission of Jesus as stated in Matthew 28:19-20 in order to teach others that they, too, might become disciples. Thus, the Church's responsibility, particularly to the urban, African-American community will be examined through these lenses.

The Church was known as an institution of teaching

and learning biblically and historically. It was not to be recognized as "God's building," but rather, as "God's people." In the Old Testament, the Israelites (who were recognized as God's chosen people) gathered to hear the Word of God through the Law of Moses (or the Pentateuch). God's commandments were also to be taught and passed on from generation to generation in the home as foretold by the prophet Moses according to the following passage:

> *"Now this is the commandment, and these are the statutes and judgments which the Lord your God has commanded to teach you, that you may observe them in the land which you are crossing over to possess, that you may fear the Lord your God, to keep all His statutes and His commandments which I command you, you and your son and your grandson, all the days of your life, and that your days may be prolonged. Therefore hear, O Israel, and be careful to observe it, that it may be well with you, and that you may multiply greatly as the Lord God of your fathers has promised you—'a land flowing with milk and honey.' "Hear, O Israel: The Lord our God, the Lord is one! You shall love the Lord your God with all your heart, with all your soul, and with all your strength. "And these words which I command you today shall be in your heart. You shall teach them diligently to your children, and shall talk of them when you sit in your house, when you walk by the way, when you lie down, and when you rise up. You shall bind them as a sign on your hand,*

and they shall be as frontlets between your eyes. You shall write them on the doorposts of your house and on your gates."

—Deuteronomy 6:1-9 (NKJV)

Those who heeded God's directive through Moses to teach His commandments to perpetual generations did so. The teaching/learning process continued in homes, temples, and synagogues from the Old Testament age of Judaism to the New Testament age of Christianity. Jesus solidified the mission of the church in His commission to the disciples to continue to "teach all nations" according to Matthew 28:19-20.

The mission or message of the Church has not changed; however, the conventional methods of evangelism must be augmented if they are to be effective in today's society. An innovative, culturally sensitive approach must be taken in order to reach the multitudes that are in the valley of decision. The Gospel of Jesus Christ must be presented in a way that is relevant to those who are seeking answers to the pervading malaise of anxiety and despair. These and other conditions must be targeted through programs that are appealing to the senses. Hence, there must be a concerted effort taken by the religious community to understand that "sight" and "sound" appeal to the generation of the twenty-first century. The method of evangelism (or teaching through Christian education), should be communicated contemporarily so as to stimulate the mind through what is seen and heard. Stimulation of the mind by way of this method leads to motivation of the will. Additionally, the message of the Gospel must be made applicable to what persons are confronted with on a daily basis. Therefore, the Church must rally together (outside of its four walls) and embrace the fact that there is a demand for contemporary or modern ministry among the disenfranchised.

Communicating the Vision

If a congregation is to take the mission of reaching the disenfranchised seriously, the pastor must make active evangelism in their surrounding community a priority by structuring it into the vision of the church. There should be uneasiness associated with the status quo of traditional ministry. Rather, the ministry of the church can become more contemporary in nature if church leaders communicate the idea of evangelizing urban America to the congregation. If the mission of reaching inner-city dwellers for the cause of Christ is shared from the pulpit to the pew, the congregation will take ownership of the vision and run with it. Conversations between leadership and laity will begin to revolve around this new thrust of moving beyond the comfort zone for the sake of making a difference in a targeted community. New ministries and changes in themes focusing on modern methods of evangelism will begin to take the forefront. Announcements, literature, and other visual stimuli communicating the importance of evangelism will assist the church in its mission to make disciples of those who are not being reached through the traditional means of "doing church."

Programs that may not allow active evangelism in an urban community to take place should be reshaped so that they become extroverted as opposed to introverted in nature. Although church members generally desire for their own needs to be met by "in-house' auxiliaries, it is equally important to consider addressing the needs of the community. It is also necessary to determine what sector of the African-American community is to serve as the target for evangelism, whether it is children, teenagers, young and/or middle-aged adults, or those over the age of fifty-five.

There are several ways of integrating evangelism and outreach into the mainstream of any church. One way to accomplish this is to make the atmosphere of the church a positive one by making visitors feel welcome. Everyone is given permission to minister when an ingrown church makes evangelism its outward focus. The synergy of individual skills and talents can lead to church growth as a result of making evangelism the norm. Myron Augsburger comments that, "Effective community outreach requires more than polished techniques. Meaningful outreach begins with a healthy attitude toward mission and community" (Calvin Ratz, 1990). Consequently, the needs of others are served before our own. In order for this to take place, the Church must embrace a marketplace mentality which causes it to become an extension of ministry to the community. Expertise and service are offered, rather than forced, upon a target audience. Public support is given through prayer and meaningful dialogue to ascertain specific community needs. The church's vision and mission should be directed toward a specific targeted audience, namely, the urban, African-American community.

Encouraging target-group outreach enables a church to touch those who would not otherwise be exposed to the message of Jesus Christ and the ministry of the Church through traditional methods. Frank Tillapaugh states the following:

> A target group is simply people who share a common need or experience on whom the Church focuses its outreach. Instead of broadly scattering the gospel to all people without Christ, target-group ministry aims its sights on one particular group of people with specific needs. If mass evangelism is like watering a garden with a sprinkler (which may waste some water and may not give each plant the exact amount of water it needs), target-group evangelism is like watering each plant with a hose (which not only saves water but attends to the specific needs of each plant). Target-group ministry usually springs up when someone recognizes a need no one else is meeting adequately (Calvin Ratz, *Mastering Outreach and Evangelism*, 1990).

Since the target group for evangelism is constantly being multiplied, pastors should prod and praise the congregation so that this group can be reached on a consistent basis. Pastors can do so by preaching evangelistic sermons from the pulpit. In this way, evangelism to the urban community is presented as a cooperative church effort as language and themes used connect the vision and mission of the Church to its members.

The vision of targeting the urban, African-American community for evangelism through Christian education will prove effective when the specific spiritual and practical needs of the inner-city (which have not been adequately met) are addressed. As a result, persons will be channeled into ministries of relevance because of the difference these ministries have made in their personal lives and community. Just as the military recruits and enlists people for active duty, so must the Church. Jesus made disciples of His followers so that they could take what was invested into them and impart it into the lives of others. We are to reproduce ourselves by introducing Christ and His teachings to others in our communities. We do this effectively by living in such a manner as to attract people to the Savior of the world, Jesus Christ. We prepare ourselves to witness to others through prayer, knowledge, and application of scriptural principles, personal testimony, and consistent evangelistic training. Not only must we prepare ourselves spiritually, but we also need to learn and utilize practical methods in our strategy of leading a targeted audience to salvation. However, the Holy Spirit's role in drawing people to Jesus Christ is not to be forgotten or taken lightly.

People must work in cooperation with the Holy Spirit if evangelism is to be effective. Every person has been entrusted with certain gifts and the necessary resources to accomplish their God-given purpose. Therefore, it stands to reason that every church has exactly who and what it needs to do what God has called each church to do. Each spiritual gift, natural talent, and acquired skill should be inventoried and utilized in an effort to make the vision of reaching the African-American community for the cause of Christ a reality.

Conducting Research

Many African-Americans blame Anglo-Saxons or "the system" for their present condition or socioeconomic status. On the other hand, there are many whites who either refuse to interact with blacks, or feel compelled to do so out of a sense of moral guilt. However, ministries to urban America must be more than a "guilt offering" or a Band-Aid solution applied to the pervasive conditions that continue to this present hour (Lovett, 1992). Entire congregations, whether segregated or interracial, must begin to heal the bitter wounds of the past by partnering together in an effort to produce bridge-building strategies out of a sense of love for one another, as well as for those outside of Christendom. Only then can the religious sector rise as an institution that demonstrates equality and unity among races and ethnic groups. After the Church releases any preconceived ideas or dogmas that would hinder effective evangelism to the urban, African-American community, further research can be developed.

There are many low-income families living in urban America. African-Americans and other ethnic groups falling within this category are forced to live in public housing in order to survive. The religious sector can take the first step toward evangelizing these areas by conducting a survey to ascertain and meet specific needs. A particular community, or perhaps a public school, can be targeted and researched in order to develop effective methodologies and a plan for improvement.

Church leaders with a desire to help meet the needs of those who live in seemingly impoverished communities may do so by working in conjunction with city officials such as the mayor, city council members, the city manager, and the police commissioner. A statistical analysis of a specific community can easily be obtained from a local city when it is requested if it is to be properly utilized in a positive manner. Relevant statistical data can also be accessed via the internet and used to establish programs that will benefit the community by meeting needs that exist.

Establishing Programs and Personnel

There are two major resources that are needed in order to bring restoration to the urban environment: creative programs and committed personnel. However, programs and personnel chosen must be geared toward assisting those who have been caught in the depredation of immorality and lawlessness, in an effort to demonstrate that restoration, redemption, and empowerment are available and attainable through the lordship of Jesus Christ. Therefore, one must take the call of evangelism through Christian education, as well as those who sense a mandate to become actively involved in the evangelism process, seriously.

An evangelist is recognized by most as "a revivalist or a preacher [or teacher], who holds large public services in various cities" (*Webster's New World Dictionary*, 1990). It can be assumed then, that an evangelist does not randomly present the gospel message to a public audience without first organizing a strategy so that the implementation thereof would prove to be effective. Thus, the process of revitalizing America's inner cities must begin with the stage of identifying needs within a targeted community, and creating specific programs designated to meet those needs. An example of evangelizing an urban community can be seen by visiting churches which are ministering effectively to those who live and worship in their respective areas. The demonstration of effective evangelism results in the building of bridges of trust which lead to the development of relationships birthed out of obedience to Christ and love for one another. It is incumbent upon the religious sector to become involved with an urban community in order to gain firsthand knowledge and show genuine concern to inner-city dwellers. This type of commitment will most certainly cause others to become actively involved in bridging the gap between urban and suburban communities and racial groups. Those who desire to seize such an opportunity can do the following:

- Partner with others who share their conviction and compassion for the inner city (such as other local churches in the area or persons who are already pursuing solutions and programs to meet specific needs);
- Offer their specific talents or professions to inner-city residents during after-school or evening community service programs to assist both children and adults;
- Solicit donations (whether monetary or otherwise) from entrepreneurs, local churches, other organizations and individuals in an effort to promote wholesome entertainment for adults and children with urban neighborhoods (such as small-scale carnivals,

talent shows, concerts, drama presentations, etc.) in order to counteract negative images with positive alternatives; and/or

- Conduct a survey to ascertain whether or not child care service is needed. If so, day care service and transportation for children can be provided by local churches. (This presents a tremendous opportunity for evangelism to children through Christian education, which can be further developed into an established Christian day school for the community. Financial assistance from social service agency programs and businesses, as well as grants and fundraising efforts, can be generated to support this endeavor.)

Previously conducted research in urban areas should be utilized in the program planning process. For instance, if statistics prove that there are numerous single parent homes headed by young females, an opportunity is presented to the Church to establish several types of mentoring programs. Methods could be devised to better equip young mothers to handle the responsibility of raising children properly by offering parental training courses. Employment counseling booths (which would include information concerning appropriate attire, conduct and conversation during an interview, specific job training skills, and role-playing), could be displayed within the community to pique curiosity and interest, while providing a definite avenue of empowerment. Other strategies can be geared toward meeting the immediate needs of young males without fathers in the home. Remediation classes for both adults and children could also be organized to reduce the number of functionally illiterate persons. Furthermore, local community colleges, day care facilities, financial institutions, social service agencies and civic organizations, could offer assistance by displaying information booths with resources that could prove beneficial to passersby. All of these ideas could initially take place by having what could be termed as "Community Unity Day" (which has been instituted and implemented in targeted urban communities in Hampton, Virginia by Calvary Community Church). Church members, entrepreneurs, and other interested persons, could meet with local city officials and urban residents in order to plan such an event.

The aforementioned programs, as well as a host of others, could take place within urban area homes or at a nearby community center as an extension of the local church. These practical ways of meeting individual needs through creative programs serve as a prelude to introducing the gospel message. The poignancy of meeting such needs is more clearly expressed by Jesus Christ Himself in Matthew 42:40: "…inasmuch as ye have done it unto *(meaning to meet the needs of)* one of the least of these my brethren *(those that are disdained by society)*, ye have done it unto *(met the needs of)* me *(Jesus Christ Himself)*." This scripture implies that those whose apparent needs are being ignored by the overwhelming majority should be recognized and responded to by the Church. *(Italics and parenthetical statements are my interpretation within the context of the scriptural passage and the content of this chapter.)*

There are many persons who possess the knowledge of scripture and the ability to evangelize. A background or experience in the ministry of teaching or evangelism is in itself an invaluable source of training. Most importantly though, is the motivation for becoming involved in such a task. Compassion should be the driving force that compels the evangelist to share his/her faith with others—not remuneration, a sense of obligation, or guilt. Consequently, the knowledge of the Christian faith and the ability to present the gospel in a culturally sensitive and developmentally appropriate manner, is essential. The very heartbeat of evangelism resonates each time a person chooses to become a disciple of Christ as a result of the teaching/learning process. In fact, the importance of selecting personnel committed to this task far outweighs the programs or methods chosen.

Persons committed to the task of "soul-winning" become leaders in their own right. Their characters must exemplify integrity and moral strength that can be modeled to others. Moreover, those involved in Christian education must possess the wherewithal to effectively communicate the gospel message to indigenous urban America. This simply means that leaders or laity instrumental in empowering and evangelizing inner-city dwellers must be internally and externally equipped to do so. Therefore, it is necessary to examine the personal and professional lifestyles of those who desire to serve as modern-day missionaries to the urban community.

Whereas the formal training of the modern-day missionary should be considered, it is one's personal testimony or witness that is of vital importance to the evangelistic process. One cannot expect to whet the appetite of others to become Christian without recognizing that an individual's behavior and service to the community are standards by which persons are judged by the broader society. In fact, it has been reported that some of the main reasons why African-American men do not attend church is because of the religious community's hypocrisy, irrelevance and Eurocentric attitudes and expectations (Kunjufu, 1995). In order to refute these and other hurling accusations given by secular society, the church must focus its efforts upon rebuilding individual "Christian character," which could be defined as: having integrity (or the possession of a morally clean and honest lifestyle); loyalty (to God, family, church, and employers); and having a servant's heart (by willingly giving of one's time, talent, and treasures). Essentially, those with true Christian character act in direct opposition to the world's philosophy of "What can I get?" Instead, they are willing to serve in capacities that are considered by many as beyond the call of duty by asking "What can I give?" It is this desire to serve others that internally motivates the evangelist to present the gospel message, without biased personal opinions or thoughts.

Persons who are interested in evangelism through Christian education should pursue further training to better enhance any innate abilities or skills. Formal instruction can be administered by a pastor within a church setting or by other qualified personnel through Bible college and seminary programs. Degrees can be obtained from the Associate to the Doctorate level in such areas as Christian Theology, Ministry, Education, Counseling or Psychology. Specific external degree programs especially designed for pastors and other full-time church leaders can be utilized by those who are unable to leave their places of employment and other responsibilities to attend on-site classes. Certain schools also offer pastors and church leaders the opportunity to submit ministry resumes, and the school may choose to award credits for lifetime experience which can be applied toward a degree.

Additionally, tuition costs at Christian colleges may be lower when compared to a secular institution.

Although years of formal study help to prepare and refine the task of teaching or evangelism, it is the sense of an inner call from God that solidifies that task. There are many teachers, but only a few of them possess the gift to teach. Perhaps Matthew 20:16 can be applied to the task of teaching as well: *"…for many are called, but few chosen."* The teacher must be thoroughly prepared as well as qualified to teach. It is not necessarily the degree itself or certification from one's state that makes the teacher.

The Christian educator must recognize that there are certain attitudes that must prevail in order for effective teaching to take place. First and foremost, the teacher must take the task of teaching as well as the students seriously. The instructor should never be ill prepared or haphazard in his or her approach to teaching. Second, the teacher needs to have a desire for his or her students to learn upon delivery of the subject material. Third, an attitude showing that the teacher has a desire for the students to experience authentic Christian community must be evident. This means that the teacher will introduce the student to ways of connecting with other believers.

There are three components within each individual that must be reached if effective teaching is to occur: the mind, the heart and the will. It is with the mind that we receive and process information. Therefore, the teacher must purposefully stimulate the intellect of the learner on an appropriate level. The heart represents the emotions or feelings; thus, it is incumbent upon the teacher to present the lesson in a manner which will cause the learner to respond with his or her heart.

Last, the will consists of the ability to do or to act. Hence, the will is directly related to what is perceived with the mind, as well as what is felt with the heart. Consequently, the teacher must present the lesson in a way that will cause the student to know, feel, and do that which relates to the Word of God. Creative Christian education programs coupled with committed personnel dedicated to the tasks of teaching and evangelizing are the remedies to the adverse conditions prevalent in our society. In an effort to reach the world for Christ, one must not neglect the immediate surroundings which serve as fertile missionary soil. Before the uttermost parts of the earth can be claimed for God, the inner cities of Jerusalem, Judea, and Samaria must be targeted (Acts 1:8). One should begin to evangelize neighboring families and communities as a matter of priority. One of the most effective programs for reaching inner-city dwellers and their progeny for generations to come is the establishment of a Christian day care center and school.

7
Establishing a Christian Day Care Center and School

STARTING A CHRISTIAN day care center and school is not as difficult as some might believe. However, it requires a great deal of patience and persistence in order to see the task through to the end. Many may try to dissuade persons from establishing such programs as an extension of the local church to the community. Edger A. Guest penned the attitude that Christians should have in accomplishing feats in the face of ridicule or doubt in the following poem.

Somebody Said It Couldn't Be Done

*Somebody said it couldn't be done, but he,
with a chuckle replied
That maybe it couldn't, but he would be one who wouldn't
say so till he'd tried.
He waded right in with a trace of a grin on his face;
if he worried, he did it.
He started to sing as he tackled the thing that couldn't
be done—and he did it.
Somebody said, "Oh, you'll never do that,
at least no one ever has done it."
But he took off his coat and he took off his hat;
and the first thing we know, he'd begun it.
With a lift of the chin and a bit of a grin,*

> *without any doubting or "quit it,"*
> *He started to sing as he tackled the thing that*
> *couldn't be done—and he did it.*
> *There are thousands to tell you it cannot be done,*
> *there are thousands to prophesy failure.*
> *There are thousands to point out to you, one by one,*
> *the dangers that wait to assail you.*
> *But just buckle in with a lift of the chin,*
> *take off your coat and go to it.*
> *Starting to sing as you tackle the thing that cannot be done—*
> *and you'll do it.*
> (Baker, *The Successful Christian School*, 1990)

The necessity of starting a Christian day care center and school is actually recognized by all who agree that America's public school system in many respects has failed in its attempt to produce literate, articulate youth who are prepared for institutions of higher learning. In secular schools, most Christians will concur that there is simply no place for God in the system. School prayer and an awareness, if not an acceptance of God, has been replaced by the new god of diversity which seemingly respects all world views and philosophies except those from the Judeo-Christian heritage. Not only is the Christian perspective excluded from the classroom, but it is often ridiculed and undermined as well. Furthermore, the dominant philosophies of relativism (which categorically denies the existence of truth or moral absolutes) and political correctness (which allows persons to advocate or express only the ideas that are held and approved by broader society), pervade the public school system. In fact, many secular schools—from elementary to institutions of higher learning—have become breeding grounds for sexual promiscuity, homosexuality, unwanted pregnancies, abortions, alcoholism, and drug abuse (Dobson, 1995). As a result of the negative conditions that exist in the public education domain, many parents seek to enroll their children in private institutions. Hence, the Christian school movement is growing at an incredible rate both nationally and internationally. The Association of Christian Schools International (ACSI) presently claims a membership of well over 1,500 schools. The growth pattern of the Christian school movement is phenomenal.

Is there a new demand for Christian education as parents, teachers and the church partner together in this effort, especially amongst society's youth and successive generations in urban America? The posing of this rhetorical question should provoke all Christians to immediate action. The investment into the lives of children and their families by those who heed such a demand will yield internal, external, and eternal rewards as countless youth are introduced to character training and academic excellence from a biblical perspective. This is definitely an alternative to secular, humanistic education.

Counting the Cost

The advantages of offering Christian education through day care and school programs are unparalleled. However, one should carefully consider the feasibility and costs of such a venture. There is no set amount of capital required to start a Christian day care or school. The cost is contingent upon the number of grades or programs offered, the availability and usage of a building and furniture (whether new, used or on-hand), administrative and faculty salaries, curriculum and promotional materials, and other necessary resources or equipment needed to meet local, state, and/or federal codes and compliances. These figures will assist in determining the priority of needs to be met in order to operate a Christian day care center and school both effectively and efficiently.

    The initial decision concerning the locale of day care and school programs is essential. Church facilities usually provide the best facilities for beginning centers. For instance, Sunday school rooms and the nursery could easily be converted into day care and school classrooms. Chalkboards, bulletin boards, desks, tables, chairs, and other classroom furniture can be utilized temporarily until new purchases can be made. Other supplies such as flags, easels, flannel boards, toys, books, puzzles, computers, and mats or cots for sleeping, may be readily available in a church facility as well. Moreover, most churches already have adequate kitchen and bathroom facilities which only need to be adjusted on a small scale, for the most part, in order to meet local or state building, health, and sanitary codes. The church council or board members could also be instrumental in operating the day care and school by agreeing to provide counsel, direction, and financial assistance through a subsidy given by faithful congregants who align themselves with the vision of Christian education.

    Lunch and transportation programs are not necessary at the beginning stage of starting a Christian day care or school. Costs for the lunch program can be defrayed by instituting a "bag or box lunch" policy. If all prospective students bring their lunches, there is no need for food service preparations or personnel. Parents may also be encouraged to bring fruit, crackers or juice for nursery and/or preschool snack times. Additionally, transportation can be avoided as well by encouraging parents to car pool. If church leaders agree to lend use of their vehicles, one or two buses picking up groups of children can be done effectively. Perhaps other churches in the area which support the idea of starting a Christian day care or school may agree to provide bus transportation for the community as well.

Salaries and other overhead expenses, as mentioned previously, vary. Small schools generally cannot afford a full-time principal the first year or two. The pastor of the church or one of the half-day teachers, designated as a head teacher, may be used to fill that position instead. The teacher's salary must be determined by the pastor and/or governing board. If salaries are kept low, tuition costs can be kept low to better ensure that more people from the community as well as the church can afford to send their children to a Christian day care center and school. Consequently, the administration's salary should not greatly exceed the salary of the teachers. Other overhead expenses, such as janitorial costs, can be avoided if teachers and responsible students keep their classrooms clean. Trash receptacles can be emptied, floors can be swept or vacuumed, and boards can be cleaned. Overhead expenses may also be borne by the church until the school can pay its own way.

Local community residents and church members can become actively involved by physically and financially supporting the quest to begin a Christian day care center and school as the vision is promoted in a positive, enthusiastic manner. The need for Christian education as an alternative to the effects of secular humanism can be expressed in various ways. A group meeting with a kick-off carnival, banquet, or special service with a guest speaker, could be held in a local church or on the streets of a targeted community. The anticipation of such a meeting may cause a spark that further ignites a blaze of excitement among attendees. Moreover, an inexpensive yet attractive flier or brochure, can be designed and distributed in order to advertise the location, low tuition costs, and quality Christian education programs that are to be offered.

There are many resources that are available to aid the process of ascertaining costs and selecting personnel and programs in order to start a Christian day care center and school. Numerous books on Christian education can be easily attained and utilized to assist in this endeavor. There are also local, state and regional conferences that can be attended in order to gain a better understanding of the educational process. Textbook publishers and distributors can also offer assistance in introducing and explaining the mechanics of their respective curricula. Additionally, there are in depth clinics held annually for principals, supervisors, office managers and teachers in April, August and November at Pensacola Christian College located in Pensacola, Florida. Dr. Arlin and Beka Horton, founders of the A Beka curriculum, Pensacola Christian Schools (including nursery through high school) and Pensacola Christian College, share personal advice, wisdom, and experiences during these seminar sessions in an effort to equip attendees for the task of ministry in a Christian school setting. There are yet many more avenues of acquiring inspirational, professional and practical information, including accreditation—among them being other successful Christian schools, and state or national conferences hosted by Christian organizations such as the Association of Christian Schools International (ACSI), Accrediting Commission International (ACI) and others.

Information for Religiously Exempt Centers

Information concerning the submittal of required documentation and adherence to restricted code compliances in order to operate a day care center and/or school may differ from state to state. However, because of the separation between church and state, it is highly recommended that day care centers and schools operated by religious institutions file for exemption from licensure. In such cases, religious institutions are given the freedom to teach subject content from a Christian perspective without state interference. This by no means suggests that churches without state licensure are not required to meet or exceed the state's standards for operating day care centers or private, religious schools. As a matter of fact, such institutions must file specific documentation with the Department of Social Services and undergo various inspections to ensure that they are operating in full accordance with state code requirements for religiously exempt centers. Failure to do so will result in the suspension or revocation of a religious institution's exemption from licensure status.

According to applicable codes in Virginia, exempt child day centers operating under the auspices of a religious institution must submit required documentation annually to the licensing offices of the Department of Social Services. The documents are described as follows:

- A Statement of Intent (conveying intent to begin or continue to operate a child day care center)
- Certification of Tax Exempt Status (including a statement from a local tax commissioner's or real estate assessor's office that the property owned and exclusively operated by the religious institution is exempt from local taxation, or a statement from the Internal Revenue Service that the religious institution is tax exempt as a non-profit religious organization under Section 501(c)(3) of the Internal Revenue Code)
- A Local Health Report/Report of Sanitary Inspection
- A Local Health Report/Food Establishment Inspection Report
- A Local Fire Report
- The Building Inspector's Report/Certificate of Occupancy or State Fire Marshal's Report
- Verification of Required Staff/Child Ratios
- Staff Health Reports
- A Statement of Code Compliance (disclosing certain information to the parents or guardians of the children in the center and the general public)

According to the Virginia State Code, the sponsoring religious institution must comply by providing specific information or assurance to parents or guardians of children enrolled and the general public concerning the center's licensure, general staff qualifications, physical facilities, enrollment capacity, food service offered, staff health requirements, public liability insurance, criminal history record checks and the establishment and implementation of other staff policies and procedures as warranted.

After submitting all of the above documentation to the Department of Social Services, the religious institution must receive confirmation that it is in compliance with the State Code to operate a child day care center and/or school. At this point, a letter is issued from the agency granting religious exemption from state licensure for a period of one year after the date that the documentation was received. The same documentation and inspection reports must be filed annually except for certain specified information that is only required at the initial filing for exemption from licensure. This is a lengthy process, but the dividend of making an eternal difference in the lives of children and their families through Christian education, is well worth the investment.

Choosing a Curriculum

The quality of a Christian day care center and/or school and its continued growth in the future, depends largely upon a sound philosophy of Christian education, committed and qualified personnel, and a proven curriculum based upon Biblical precepts, a standard of excellence, and common sense. The objective for choosing material to be taught in a Christian day setting must be measured against the standard that a particular school is to uphold. This will determine whether the road to mediocrity or excellence is taken. Therefore, the definition of a curriculum and its effectiveness must be researched and analyzed.

"A curriculum is a plan by which the teaching/learning process may be systematically undertaken" (Wyckoff, 1961). It can be assumed from this definition then, that the evaluator of a curriculum in question must take into account specific "goals, [a] plan, [a] design, materials, teachers, [and] methods" (Eleanor Daniel J. W., *Introduction to Christian Education*, 1987). Certainly the components found in John Milton Gregory's book entitled *The Seven Laws of Teaching*, lend themselves to the process of choosing a curriculum as well. These seven elements (the teacher, the student, the lesson, the teacher's work, the student's work, a common language, and review) must be designed into the curriculum so that effective instruction can take place in a Christian environment.

The teacher must be prepared and equipped with the knowledge and resources necessary to communicate subject material to the student on a developmentally-appropriate level. The teacher, the subject material, and the classroom methods, should be able to capture the attention and interest of the learner, causing him or her to respond in a manner that denotes cognitive, social, and spiritual growth. The curriculum should also provide sufficient time for review before new material is introduced. This will enable the teacher to measure a student's ability to comprehend, as well as grant an opportunity to teach and reinforce previous concepts in an innovative manner.

There are a number of excellent curriculum kits that are available which include user-friendly lesson plans complete with textbooks, teacher manuals and visual aids. Several publishing companies offer curriculum programs ranging from preschool to high school subject material. However, it is suggested that one's philosophy of education (whether progressively secular or Christian) be considered when choosing a curriculum. This will even assist in determining whether one's focus should be upon teaching sight reading and rote memorization (as derived from the progressive or modern education movement) or teaching intensive phonics and critical thinking skills (as was traditionally done in Christian schools). Consequently, the curriculum chosen should reflect the beliefs, goals, and standards of the Christian day care center and/or school.

Setting Policies and Procedures

An organization and its employees cannot function properly if responsibilities and company policies are not outlined and adhered to. In the same respect, a Christian day care center and/or school cannot operate efficiently and effectively without having information that administration, faculty and support staff, students, and their parents abide by. Hence, it becomes the responsibility of the pastor/administrator or a designated appointee, to gather the information to be utilized in the policy-making process. Once policies and regulations regarding the day care center and/or school are made, they must be put into manual form. Thus, administrative staff, faculty and other employees, as well as prospective parents and students, will be well informed of all programs and expectations. Consider developing the following manuals while incorporating specific goals that can be realistically accomplished in a Christian setting (using suggestions made as a result of my first-hand knowledge in personally developing, refining, testing, and teaching this and other information to Christian school administrators, supervisors, office staff, and faculty):

- A Student Handbook for day care and/or elementary students could contain information regarding programs for specific ages; before/after school care; a scope and sequence curriculum overview; a list of necessary school supplies; testing and evaluation procedures; school arrival and dismissal times; policies on behavior, discipline, suspensions, expulsions and withdrawals; conferences, parent-teacher groups and newsletters; meals and snacks; health procedures and physical education; special fees, etc.

- An Employee Handbook could consist of information regarding administrative policies; annual academic school year and summer contracts; employee recruitment, selection, placement, advancement opportunities, vacancies and nepotism; classification of employees (full-time, part-time, salaried or volunteer); probationary appointment; work week descriptions; compensation; attendance, punctuality and absences; employee benefits; codes regarding dress, ethics, conduct and confidentiality; lunch breaks, etc.

- An Office Procedure Manual can consist of information regarding time clock and telephone procedures; personal mail; confidentiality; the collection of tuition and social service payments; delinquent accounts; how to conduct a parent tour; school registration; annual exemption from licensure renewal; health and fire inspections and fire drills; and miscellaneous forms for administrative, faculty and office use.

- A Supervisors' Training Manual can be comprised of information which would assist supervisors in making a smooth transition to supervision; overcoming the early problems of leadership; developing listening skills and methods to plan, set goals, produce, instruct, assign and delegate tasks; developing the means to choose a leadership style and motivational techniques that will help in avoiding common mistakes in order to build a positive work environment and dispel negative attitudes; making changes, pinpointing problems, and having face-to-face discussions; and observing/evaluating others.

- A Teacher/Staff Procedure Manual can provide information concerning the philosophy of Christian education; teacher observation/evaluation tips; grading scales and classroom schedules; assertive discipline techniques and basic classroom habits and procedures; creative activities for young children; and appendices including miscellaneous forms, advice for teaching, back-to-school orientation and in-service training notes.

Even though the Christian philosophy of education differs from that of the secular realm, it is vitally important to keep abreast of recent developments in both arenas. Administrators and faculty members from religiously owned and operated centers or schools can become involved in Christian and secular organizations which offer programs for membership and/or accreditation in an attempt to network with other schools and leaders in the educational field. Many workshops are held to demonstrate the effective use of curriculum materials while offering professional development and inspiration as well. A subscription to the Association of

Supervision and Curriculum Development (ASCD) will also assist in relaying the most recent developments in public as well as private education, such as, computer technology and how to integrate age-appropriate software into the curriculum; the latest National Council of Teachers of Mathematics (NCTM) standards; multiple intelligences; reading and learning styles and teaching methods geared toward them; integrated, thematic and cooperative learning strategies; literacy assessment techniques; and inclusion. It is also recommended to contact the state board of education in order to receive the standards of learning against which to measure the effectiveness of the chosen curriculum at each grade level to ensure that minimum standards are met and surpassed.

Although meeting the academic needs of the students enrolled in a Christian school is important, it should not take precedence over the spiritual training which is so vitally needed. For the Christian educator, the most important subject to be taught is the Bible. Every lesson, irrespective of the topical study, should be based upon the foundation of God's Holy Word. Stories may be used to illustrate or illuminate the lesson, but the principles taught are from the Bible, and should be taught with conviction and exuberance. The teacher must proclaim the lesson in such a fashion that the hearer is convinced of its authenticity. The ability to do so stems from an intimate relationship with God. The teacher who is energized by having such a relationship is able to teach with the excitement that comes from knowing God and having a lifestyle based on biblical principles.

Evaluating Faculty

All teachers must plan for the immediate future through the use of short-term goals and lesson plans. Yet, there remains another perspective that comes with the territory of teaching—the evaluation. This tool allows one to structure and adopt specific goals that will lead to effective teaching strategies. Howard Hendricks states it best: "Experience in teaching doesn't tend to sharpen [the teacher's] abilities; rather it dulls them. It is evaluated experiences that improve [a teacher's] skills (*Mastering Teaching*, 1991).

Many who instruct others may be reluctant concerning models of evaluation for several reasons. They may not want to face the possible reality of not connecting the lessons taught to the students; thus, the very thought of being ineffective may chip away at the teacher's sense of self-worth or esteem. It could be that those who are hesitant have not learned to accept the constructive criticism or to acknowledge the biases of others. Many may even think that no one has the right to evaluate them, for they view evaluation as judgment from men, which, in their opinion, has no place in Christendom; that is God's business alone, they would say. Nevertheless, those who teach must constantly scrutinize themselves, making sure that they are teaching effectively and that their students are grasping and applying the lessons taught. While self-evaluation is necessary, team support in the form of constructive criticism and appraisals from trusted friends in the teaching profession (and from students themselves) is crucial. The teacher who adheres to the evaluation process is a teacher who is secure. Their desire is to not only teach, but to teach well.

The model used for evaluation should examine several

areas. Particularly in the case of a Christian educator, the tool used should measure whether or not goals set by the teacher have been met: the students should have been pointed toward Jesus in an effort to live more like Christ. If the students are not perfected in Him and better equipped to serve in ministry as a result of being taught the Word, something is wrong. Either the teacher has not effectively communicated biblical principles, or the students have refused to apply the principles taught. In an effort to analyze which of these scenarios holds true, the Christian educator should seek to answer these three questions: What did I do well? What did I do poorly? What changes should I make?

Although teaching can be one of the most personally gratifying and rewarding professions that there is, it seems to be one of the most underpaid and disregarded occupations in society. Teachers are expected to give willingly and effortlessly of their time and talents without regard for remuneration or public acknowledgment. This underlying sentiment may be the cause of the steady decline of teachers and volunteers in both the public and private sector. Many administrators would probably agree that it is difficult to recruit and keep quality teachers, especially without some sort of incentive.

Quality is never to be sacrificed, and the Christian day care and school is no exception. The pastor, administrator and/or committee who have been given the responsibility of recruitment should interview persons who are gifted to teach and profess to be Christians. The prospective candidates should possess a desire to serve rather than a desire to be served. Their lives should display the love of Christ and adherence to biblical principles. The candidates should understand the difference between a vocation and an occupation. A vocation has to do with a person's calling or the election of a person to answer and heed the call of God upon one's life. In contrast, an occupation is the career or path that a person chooses that leads to financial success. In other terms, an occupation is simply employment that allows you to pay the bills, but a vocation is a passion that one pursues without thought of monetary gain in order to fulfill one's purpose in life. Herein is the difference between a job and a ministry.

The recruitment team should allow the prospective teaching candidates time to process and discern the will of God in accepting a ministry position without guilt or manipulation. They should be given a job description which outlines their duties in the ministry. The vision and expectations of the ministry should also be clearly articulated so that there will be unity amongst those who are newly and currently employed. Of course, after the interview process has been completed, the work of the Holy Spirit upon the hearts of the prospective candidates and those who have the responsibility of hiring them must prevail. Although questions have been asked and answered and applications and resumes have been meticulously screened, it is prayer and the Holy Spirit's leading that must take precedence.

There are times in the recruitment process when those who are interviewed may choose not to accept the position. It could be that the vision and expectations of the ministry were not properly communicated, or that the prospective candidate has what may seem to be an excuse for accepting an opportunity for volunteerism or employment. For example, a person who is asked to serve as a day care assistant may not accept because he or she is a novice. If the person asked has never taught or worked with children before, he or she may feel inadequate. In this instance, the recruiter could offer assistance in the form of providing workshops or mentoring relationships in an effort to equip the prospective volunteer or employee with knowledge and experience related to the field of early childhood activities. Perhaps after becoming acquainted with the resources necessary for working with youth, the candidate may come without excuse and accept the position.

One author refers to the fact that some teachers may exhibit signs of The Elijah Syndrome. Tell tale signs include "a sense of energy depletion, dissatisfaction, and malaise, often accompanied by spiritual attack in the form of self-doubt and doubting God" (*Mastering Teaching*, 1991). There were several ideas given in order to avert the signs of this syndrome from manifesting in the lives of the teaching staff. A sure way to combat this is to continue to encourage and motivate teachers and volunteers. They should be prayed for on a consistent basis and rewarded in small ways such as the giving of books, supplies, and other resources that are necessary for teaching.

There are several factors that are referred to as de-motivators in the teaching profession. If a teacher enters the classroom to find that the furniture has been rearranged, or that the supplies or equipment that he or she needs is missing, the teacher may be disappointed to say the least. Other factors may include inadequate lighting, poor ventilation, or the fact that the teacher is expected to teach those with emotional or psychological problems that he or she is not equipped to handle. To seemingly add insult to injury, the custodial duties may need to be performed by the teacher in addition to lesson preparation and instruction. There is probably an unending list of de-motivators that could never be counted. Yet this fact remains: the only way to resist the seemingly counterproductive influences or factors that exist is to allow the passion for teaching and the love of students to supersede and override everything else. The person who has accepted a position based on the call or vocation rather than a career or occupation will never lose sight of what is important, for that which is important becomes priority.

Those who heed the call of God upon their lives to teach should be expected to mentor others. In fact, this is at the heart of the Great Commission found in Matthew 28:19-20. The disciples were to pass on to others what they themselves had learned by reproducing themselves. Those who possess the gift of teaching who are in the profession for mere pleasure and reward of ministry rather than money should also have the goals of reproducing themselves in others. These are they who possess a heart for doing what they do best. In the field of Christian education, those who possess this treasure are the zealots who *should* train others.

The best teachers serve as the best trainers. Therefore, it behooves the church administration to pair the best Christian teachers with those who need to be trained in the teaching ministry. The trainer-trainee relationship should be mutually beneficial. Not only should the trainee learn from the trainer, but the trainer should purpose to learn from the trainee. The mentor should never think or feel as though he or she has nothing left to learn. There are always new heights that can be reached and methods that can be improved. In order to continue to progress as a teacher, the mentor must have the goal of observing and learning from others as well. Even though the trainer may be perceived as being "the perfect teacher," he or she must continue to employ the *PIE* approach to teaching: *Preparation, Implementation* and *Evaluation.*

The mentoring process begins when the trainee is assigned to the trainer. Once initial contact has been made, the trainer should look for and create opportunities of learning. As encouragement and disagreement are expressed regularly and openly, trust is built. Shortly thereafter, a bond is developed between the mentor and the mentee. After learning as much as possible, the trainee becomes somewhat detached from the trainer in the sense that he or she is now expected to utilize what has been learned in the classroom setting without the presence of the mentor. Thus, the mentor fades gracefully out of the relationship.

Teachers and volunteers must continue to be resourced so that the mentor-mentee relationship can continue. Opportunities for growth and advancement in the ministry should come in the form of seminars, conferences, curriculum training and the like. Church administration should make sure that the costs of such opportunities are provided for as a budget expense. In-service training opportunities may be utilized as a means of a more cost-effective approach. Other resources such as audio and visual aids as well as suggested reading material can prove to be valuable avenues of training. Teachers are to be students of lifelong learning. This simple fact encompasses the art and mastery of teaching.

Administration and Management

Those who lead others must possess certain unmistakable qualities, among them being integrity, discernment, vision, and influence. Although there are many attributes that should be seen in the life of a church leader, those previously mentioned are critical to the success of any organization. The book of Nehemiah clearly delineates the life of one who was seemingly born to lead. Nehemiah was a man of valor who was aware of the state of his people and his homeland. He knew that the gates of Jerusalem were burned and that the walls were in desperate need of repair. A God-breathed vision fueled him to garner the resources needed to inspire the people of Israel to rebuild the walls of Jerusalem. Church leaders, like Nehemiah, must also possess the ability to discern felt needs and afterward, inspire others to respond to those needs. The emergence of illiteracy and immorality in the inner city as well as in other areas and communities should be viewed as a definite need that is to be addressed by the local church and its leadership.

Although most people concentrate on the positive side of administrative and/or managerial leadership, there must be an awareness of the other end of the spectrum. Becoming a manager of people in a Christian or secular organization requires a great deal of time and energy. A leader must be well informed at all times regarding the needs of the organization, as well as the responsibilities and morale of those who work or volunteer within the organization. Time must be spent on bureaucratic details such as programs, budget reviewing and curriculum design, which may cause a manager to become somewhat detached from those he or she supervises. Equally important are the delegation of specific tasks, training of personnel, and, of course, preventing or troubleshooting problems that occur, and creating solutions. Other drawbacks include obscurity, meaning that no one may recognize or applaud one's accomplishments. However, when a leader's service is properly motivated, he or she does not constantly seek approval from men; self-effacement thereby replaces self-gratification.

Although the tasks of a leader may seem tedious at times, the value of management in ministry cannot be overstated. Those who serve in the capacity of Christian leadership are called to provide vision and direction. Proverbs 29:18 states: *"Where there is no vision* [prophetic revelation], *the people perish* [cast off restraint]." There must be a man or woman who possesses a prophetic revelation—a sense of urgency to fulfill a specific purpose or mandate given by God. Simply stated, a vision is a picture in the mind's eye of what God wants to do. When clearly communicated, a vision provides direction and momentum. Without a vision, people become as sheep without a shepherd, wandering aimlessly about.

Servant leaders are those who do not seek the platform, plaudits and prestige of men. Instead, they have an even greater ambition to please God Who called them by vocation to serve Him in word and deed. It becomes quite apparent, then, that their authority has been given by God. As a result, servant-leaders become keenly aware of the fact that they are appointed as stewards of power. Delegated power or authority to act as a steward is given by God and granted to leaders by those they serve as a fiduciary responsibility. Therefore, stewards are accountable and responsible to God and those they lead. It is important to realize that those who manage others will either positively affect or negatively infect those who are in their circle of influence. Hence, the integrity of a leader is never to be compromised or sacrificed.

Those who are called by vocation to communicate and distribute vision to the masses are pastors. They are responsible to the Chief Shepherd as stewards over the flock of God. Therefore, it is imperative that pastors remain God-focused and people-centered in order to accomplish the purpose for which they have been called. Prayer and Bible study are paramount in the life of a pastor. He or she can only be purpose-driven and directed by God when these two elements become daily necessities. In addition, the pastor must also acknowledge that administrative duties are a part of the ministerial or management role. Leith Anderson stated, "Administration does not keep pastors from people. It is people. It doesn't prevent [pastors from] serving them, it gives [them] a way to serve them" (*Mastering Teaching*, 1990).

Pastors who also serve as administrators foresee what the future holds for their respective churches, particularly if the mandate of starting a Christian day care center and school is to be accomplished. They are keepers of the vision. It is the pastor's role to pursue possibilities that will enhance and enlarge the mission of the church. Obstacles that preclude the advancement of the church's charge should be avoided. It is important for pastors to maintain a gazing eye upon what can be rather than focusing solely upon immediate demands and concerns. The late Robert Kennedy said it best: "Some people look at the way things are and ask why; others look at the way things could be and ask why not."

There are several methodologies that church leaders can utilize in an effort to promote the setting of goals in a Christian day care and school. The following specific strategies are suggested:

1. Have people think futuristically rather than in limited terms. This can be accomplished by visualizing what can or needs to be done for the next year instead of what is to be completed at the present time.
2. Provide options by studying the culture of the community that the church is to relate to, and determine the felt needs of that particular community.
3. Plan for opportunities rather than problems. The person who plans with this perspective in mind views ministry's challenges optimistically.
4. Emphasize ministry rather than structure. People are always more important than programs. In fact, the church should be depicted as an organism that produces life rather than an organization that stifles growth.
5. Become purpose-driven or future-oriented.

There are many strategies that can be implemented in order to ensure a successful Christian school ministry. The synthesizing of ideas and concepts into a strategic plan for future use is necessary; however, the need for effective leadership is essential. Every thriving business began with a visionary leader. The following scripture from Proverbs 24:3-4 (TLB) supports this statement: *"Any enterprise is built by wise planning, becomes strong through common sense, and profits wonderfully by keeping abreast of the facts."* These three principles (wise planning, common sense, and factual knowledge) will propel the church into the realm of prosperity. Purpose-driven ministries attract purpose-driven people. As a result, the philosophy of the ministry concerning its vision of evangelism through Christian education is perpetually communicated.

While the employment and training of human resources is of the utmost importance, the oversight of the church's financial condition is absolutely critical. Pastors and administrators must keep abreast of the utilization of all church funds, keeping in mind that every cent has been given sacrificially by others. The examination of budgetary income and expenditures should not be viewed as a daunting task, but rather as a stewardship. People who put their trust in leaders who are good managers of funds are willing to give all the more to the work of the ministry. In order to protect and promote the financial integrity of the church, it may become necessary to adopt certain policies and procedures. A system of checks and balances, internal and external audits, and the teaching of stewardship principles should be implemented in order to prevent the misappropriation of funds and build trust within the congregation.

Another important area of church management is the oversight of buildings and grounds. The maintenance of a church facility can do either of the following: distract or attract an individual. Just as a pastor effectively or ineffectively communicates a message to parishioners, so does the church's building and grounds. Thus, church leadership must determine what impression is to be made by the church's facilities. Although the pastor is not expected to serve as the building supervisor or custodial engineer, he or she is primarily responsible for the delegation of such tasks. Consultants can be utilized to gain insight concerning appropriate church school structures, building codes and compliances, furnishings, acoustics and other interests. Church facilities should, for the most part, be consistent with the mission or purpose of the church. The expectations of the community should also be taken into consideration.

As church leaders focus on the administrative task of operating a Christian school, growth may necessitate expansion for the future. At each plateau, strategies are to be put in place to break through the barriers. Growth and change often lead to chaos. It is not uncommon for people to resist this cataclysmic inevitability. Consequently, turmoil accompanies action, disruption results from change, and problems surface from incorporating new personnel to accommodate the ministry's growth. This growth pattern suggests that the church is making its mark on the community.

Administrators or managers must possess the same intrinsic qualities that are to be found in persons under their supervision. Such attributes consist of, but are not limited to, character, spiritual authenticity, ministry competency, and relational compatibility. Character is defined as "moral strength, reputation, status, and position" (*Webster's New World Dictionary*). One's character speaks to how one manages his or her personal life as well as to how one relates to others. Humility, courtesy, patience, and temperance are character traits that are found in the life of any noteworthy leader. However, even more important is the spiritual relationship between a leader and God. Ministry competency can be determined by a person's passion for using their talents and abilities for the kingdom of God. A certain amount of chemistry exists when a relational match is made between a ministry and a prospective employee or volunteer.

The oversight of ministry staff and volunteers is necessary if the church is to grow through the Christian education program. Ken Blanchard, the author of *Leadership* and *The One Minute Manager,* suggests that there are four stages or styles of leadership: direction, coaching, support, and delegation. The leader who directs leads an individual who may be somewhat of a novice through detailed instruction. The coaching style of leadership is used to give affirmation as well as immediate correction as often as necessary. The supporting leader provides emotional support, encouragement, advice, and correction to an individual who already knows what to do. Last, the leader who delegates turns the ministry over to an individual, while maintaining a reporting relationship, albeit less frequent than in the previously stated stages of leadership.

Another means of motivating staff is via the staff meeting. As the administrator or manager sets the agenda for such a meeting, careful attention should be given to include topics that will stimulate and equip staff members in order to foster a deeper commitment to excellence in personal as well as professional areas. Ministry is holistic in nature; therefore, the training of staff should be holistic in nature. As a result, a staff member should be challenged as a foursquare individual: spiritually, mentally, physically, and socially. About 25% of the staff meeting, on average, is to be spent on business issues such as the contemplation and communication of work that needs to be accomplished. Another 25% is to be geared toward relational issues to build unity and interpersonal relationships. However, the remaining 50% of the staff meeting is to focus on the educational training of staff for greater effectiveness in ministry.

The hiring and firing (or redirecting) of individuals for ministry should not be taken lightly. Careful forethought is to be given concerning the individual's gifts; the types of questions that need to be asked; the wages and/or benefits that the ministry can afford to offer; and the workshops or seminars that are available for the purpose of staff training. References should be sought after to ascertain a prospective candidate's compatibility with other people and organizations. This will help to determine the individual's suitability for the position offered. Most important, though, is the interviewee's personal relationship with God. All of these issues can be addressed during a formal interview, as well as in the application process.

It is important for the Christian school to maintain a personnel file for each employee and volunteer. The file should consist of data to show why a person was hired and information which supports the premise that the individual is qualified to teach. The files should be kept current with written records of administrative evaluations, observations or visits, and other pertinent information. All employee and volunteer files should be kept in a secure location so that access to the information is limited to authorized personnel only. The following is a useful checklist of items that should be in each teacher's personnel file: an application; letters of reference; personal testimony; copy of teaching credentials; college transcripts; legal clearances; employee evaluations; professional growth record; graduate transcripts; correspondence; commendations/achievements; employee requests; letters of warning and reprimand; conference notes; teacher rebuttals; and resignation or termination data (Smidderks, 1999-2000).

Being an administrator or manager of a Christian school requires many sacrifices on the part of a person who is in pursuit of operating and promoting a program of excellence. Consequently, the ministry leader must remain God-focused, people-centered, and administratively gifted. These three prerequisites will determine the effectiveness of the individual leader as well as the growth of the ministry. While some wish to find some secret elevator that travels at the speed of light in the direction of leadership, they fail to realize that they must instead climb the stairs. Each step leads to another opportunity of commitment and service for the glory of God and the greater good of others. And even though the flight of stairs may seem narrow and winding at times, there awaits an eternal reward from the Heavenly Father Who enlisted those in His army who would remain faithful to the clarion call of servant leadership before the world began.

Summary

SECULAR HUMANISM TEACHES that man is autonomous; he is the master of his own destiny, and therefore, has no need for guidance from any power outside of himself. As a result, there are no moral restraints, absolutes, or boundaries. Man decides his fate and his future within the scope of what is socially acceptable and politically correct. In stark contrast, those who teach from a Christian perspective utilize the inerrant and infallible Word of God (The Holy Bible) as the final authority upon which all lessons are based. Whereas secular education deals with the human and the present, Christian education points to the superhuman and the eternal. Conformity is not the objective for the Christian parent, educator and the Church, but rather, transformation as strategic partnerships are formed and maintained.

Christian education is the vehicle that, if driven properly, will carry others from a place of dismal despair and discontent, to a haven of healing and hope. The Church must no longer abandon its God-given commission to teach by relinquishing the authority to do so to secular humanists alone. The result of such acquiescence is apparent in the condition of today's society. Instead, the religious sector must acknowledge the fact that it must become a part of the solution, along with parents and educators, rather than the problem. Christians must become involved with the pervading issues that fill the media. One such issue is the crisis with the urban, African-American community. Now is the time for the Church to adopt the inner-city and surrounding areas as its target group. Parents, church leaders, laity, entrepreneurs, city officials, and urban community residents, must meet together in an effort to squelch the effects of genocide, homicide, narcotics, violence, promiscuity and illiteracy through creative programs and personnel committed to evangelism via Christian education, as well as to improve the American public school system.

There are many programs that can serve to mentor inner-city adults. Still, there must be a conscious effort to reach the youth and those yet to be born. The establishment of a Christian day care center and school can accomplish the task of evangelism and empowerment to better serve urban areas. J. P. Wickersham echoes the sentiment that parents, educators, and the Church should have in regards to their children, as well as adopted children and families from the urban environment:

> Parents (as well as surrogate parents), have too deep an interest in the welfare, especially the moral and religious welfare, of their children, to allow the sacred trust of their education, for which God will hold them responsible, to pass from their hands into those of State authorities who are cold and distant, and who, looking only at the results of their schemes upon masses of children, are apt to be regardless of their effect upon individuals. An educational agency should commence with individuals and go up to masses, for

if it commences with masses it will scarcely get down to individuals. That cannot be considered a right system of education which provides a great educational mill into whose hopper all children are thrown, and, when each has been subjected to the same grinding process, hands them back again to society. At the best, State schools can only educate the head; their machinery is much too clumsy to reach the heart (Wickersham, 1868).

It is the heart that must be touched and guarded, for from the heart flow the issues of life. The myriad of negativity portrayed by the press, is merely the clarion call of the human heart. When parents, educators, and the Church listen to this call with implication of attention and the purpose of acting with conviction, the sound will be heard and solutions will be created to ensure the spiritual, intellectual, physical, and social well-being of our children. The heart cry is simple—there is a new demand to both parent and partner with purpose, and it takes the entire village to include our homes, schools, and churches, to make such partnerships possible and successful.

The Most Important Step to becoming a Great Christian Educator

As emphasized throughout this book, the purpose of a Christian education for our youth is not merely to inform them mentally, but to transform them spiritually through a saving knowledge of Jesus Christ. As a parent, mentor, or educator, your walk with Christ is most important, as your example will impact your children or students for years to come. If you have not begun a personal relationship with Jesus Christ, read below to find out how you can do so today:

1. **Accept the fact that you are a sinner, and that you have broken God's law.** The Bible says in Ecclesiastes 7:20: *"For there is not a just man upon earth that doeth good, and sinneth not."* Romans 3:23: *"For all have sinned and come short of the glory of God."*

2. **Accept the fact that there is a penalty for sin.** The Bible states in Romans 6:23: *"For the wages of sin is death..."*

3. **Accept the fact that you are on the road to hell.** Jesus Christ said in Matthew 10:28: *"And fear not them which kill the body, but are not able to kill the soul: but rather fear him which is able to destroy both soul and body in hell."*

The Bible says in Revelation 21:8: *"But the fearful, and*

unbelieving, and the abominable, and murderers, and whoremongers and sorcerers, and idolaters, and all liars, shall have their part in the lake which burneth with fire and brimstone: which is the second death."

4. **Accept the fact that you cannot do anything to save yourself!** The Bible states in Ephesians 2:8, 9: *"For by grace are ye saved through faith: and that not of yourselves: it is the gift of God. Not of works, lest any man should boast."*

5. **Accept the fact that God loves you more than you love yourself, and that He wants to save you from hell.** *"For God so loved the world, that He gave His only begotten Son, that whosoever believeth in Him should not perish, but have everlasting life"* (John 3:16).

6. With these facts in mind, please repent of your sins, believe on the Lord Jesus Christ and pray and ask Him to come into your heart and save you this very moment.

The Bible states in the book of Romans 10:9, 13: *"That if thou shalt confess with thy mouth the Lord Jesus, and shalt believe in thine heart that God hath raised Him from the dead, thou shalt be saved." "For whosoever shall call upon the name of the Lord shall be saved."*

7. If you are willing to trust Christ as your Savior please pray with me the following prayer:

> Heavenly Father, I realize that I am a sinner and that I have sinned against you. For Jesus Christ's sake, please

forgive me of all of my sins. I now believe with all of my heart that Jesus Christ died, was buried, and rose again for me. Lord Jesus, please come into my heart, save my soul, change my life, and fill me with your Holy Spirit today. Amen.

Bibliography

American Heritage Electronic Dictionary (Third Edition), Houghton Mifflin Company, 1992.

Augsberger, Myron, Ratz, Calvin & Tillapaugh, Frank, *Mastering Outreach and Evangelism*, Christianity Today, Inc., Multnomah Press, Portland, OR, 97266, 1990.

Baker, A. A., *The Successful Christian School*, A Beka Book Publications, Pensacola, FL, 32523, Revised 1990.

Blanchard, Kenneth H. & Johnson, Spencer, *The One Minute Manager*, William Morrow & Company, Inc, New York, NY, 10019, 1981, 1982.

Bogert, Carroll, "White Ghetto?" "Newsweek", May 30, 1994, Newsweek, Inc. New York, NY.

Cousins, Don, Anderson, Leith & DeKruyter, Arthur, *Mastering Church Management*, Christianity Today, Inc., Multnomah Press, Portland, OR, 97266, 1990.

Covey, Stephen R., *The Seven Habits of Highly Effective Families*, Simon & Schuster UK, Ltd., London, WC2B 6AH, 1999.

Daniel, Eleanor, Wade, John W. & Gresham, Charles,

Introduction to Christian Education, The Standard Publishing Company, Cincinnati, OH, 88591, 1987.

Dobson, Dr. James, "The Case for Christian Colleges", "Charisma & Christian Life", September 1995, Volume 21, Number 2, Strang Communications Company, Lake Mary, FL.

Electronic Arts 3D Atlas 1.1 Macintosh CD Rom, "United States Urbanization—Percentage of Population in Big Cities", & "United States Urbanization—Total Persons in Big Cities", The Multimedia Corp., Ltd., 1994.

Franklin, Robert M., *Crisis in the Village: Restoring Hope in African-American Communities*, Fortress Press, Minneapolis, MN, 55330, 2007.

Fremont, Walter G. & Trudy, "Family Unity, Parental Involvement, and Student Success", "Balance", Volume 15, Number 1, September 1995, Bob Jones University, Greenville, South Carolina.

Gangel, Kenneth O. & Benson, Warren S., *Christian Education: Its History & Philosophy*, Moody Press, Moody Bible Institute of Chicago, 1983.

Getz, Gene, *Sharpening the Focus of the Church*, Moody Press, Moody Bible Institute of Chicago, 1974.

Gregory, John Milton, *The Seven Laws of Teaching*, Baker Book House Company, March 1991.

"Guns Rampant in Inner-City Schools, New Study Reveals", "Jet", January 10, 1993, Volume 85, Number 10, Johnson Publishing Company, Inc., Chicago, IL.

Kunjufu, Jawanza, "Why Most Black Men Don't Go to Church" from *Adam! Where Are You?* "Urban Family", Summer 1995, John M. Perkins Foundation for Reconciliation and Development, Inc., Jackson, MS.

Lovett, Leonard, "The Fire Next Time", "Ministries Today", September/October 1992, Volume 10, Number 5, Strang Communications Company, Lake Mary, FL.

McBirnie, Robert S., "Assessing the Inadequacy of the Present System of Education" in Paul A. Kienel's *The Philosophy of Christian School Education*, The Association of Christian Schools International, Whittier, CA.

Palmer, Earl, Hendricks, Howard & Hestenes, Roberta, *Mastering Teaching*, Christianity Today, Inc., Multnomah Press, Portland, OR, 97266, 1991.

Parker, Jennifer, "Book Satchel: Value-Neutral Education is No Solution", "Urban Family", Spring 1994, John M. Perkins Foundation for Reconciliation and Development, Inc., Jackson, MS.

Perkins, John, "Love Can Build A Bridge", "Charisma & Christian Life", June 1995, Volume 20, Number 11, Strang Communications Company, Lake Mary, FL.

Powers, Bruce P., *Christian Education Handbook: Resources for Church Leaders*, Broadman Press, Nashville, TN, 1981.

Salzer, James, "Faith in Public Schools Fades: Growing Support for Privatization," "The Florida Times-Union Metro," www.jacksonville.com/tuonline/stories/100299/met_1b1Priva.html.

Schmoke, The Honorable Kurt L., "Why School Vouchers Can Help Inner-City Children," Civic Bulletin 20 in pdf format, Adobe Acrobat Reader required, www.manhattan-institute.org/html/cb_20.htm.

Smidderks, Dr. Gary, "What Should Be in a Teacher File?" "Christian School Education", The Association of Christian Schools International, Volume 3, Issue 1, 1999-2000.

The 1995 Grolier Multimedia Encyclopedia, Macintosh CD Rom, "The Inner City", Grolier Electronic Publishing, Inc., 1995.

The Holy Bible (The King James Version, New King James Version, Amplified, Message and Living Bible translations)

Webster's New World Dictionary, Simon & Schuster, Inc., Warner Books, New York, NY 10020, 1990.

Webster's New World Dictionary, Warner Books Paperback Edition, Simon & Schuster, Inc., Cleveland, OH, 44114, 1990.

WORDsearch 8 Thompson Chain-Reference Bible Library CD Rom, Bible Software for Windows, 2009.

Wyckoff, D. Campbell, *Theory and Design of Christian Education Curriculum*, Westminster Press, 1961.

Contact Dr. Natalie A. Francisco

To register for a Women of Worth & Worship session offered onsite or online which includes eight-week sessions with intensive teaching utilizing either of her books (*Wisdom for Women of Worth & Worship* or *Parenting and Partnering with Purpose*) as the curriculum guide:
Dr. Natalie A. Francisco
Women of Worth & Worship, LLC
P. O. Box 9853
Chesapeake, VA 23321
Via email: wowwi@nataliefrancisco.com

To visit the Women of Worth & Worship, LLC website:
www.nataliefrancisco.com.

To request Dr. Natalie A. Francisco for church, educational or corporate speaking engagements, conferences or consultations, or to inquire about Calvary Christian Academy and its programs:
Dr. Natalie A. Francisco
Calvary Community Church & Christian Academy
2311 Tower Place
Hampton, VA 23666
(757) 825-1133
email: wowwi@calvarycommunity.org
websites: www.calvarycommunity.org
www.cca.calvarycommunity.org

To visit Dr. Francisco's book websites:
www.wisdomforwomenofworthandworship.com
www.parentingandpartneringwithpurpose.com

Made in the USA
Charleston, SC
21 May 2012